Foreword by
Florence Littauer

As someone who struggles to balance my checkbook and thinks that proper money management means shopping at sales, I was thrilled to find Rosemarie Patterson's simple and doable approach to money management. This book is for people who are like me and don't find managing their financial affairs to be easy.

If I was a financial wizard, I wouldn't need a book on money management. Books I have picked up in the past that are designed to help me be wiser with my money have been so full of technical talk that only a financial wizard could understand them. They seem to be written for the person who doesn't need help.

Rosemarie has done a masterful job of blending her years of experience as a bankruptcy attorney with practical and even fun advice that will keep you out of bankruptcy. She'll even help get you ahead. She uses fascinating real-life stories of people who thought they needed to file bankruptcy, but, with Rosemarie's guidance, were able to give themselves a "money makeover" and salvage both their credit and their personal value instead.

I am especially intrigued with Rosemarie's use of the popular personality principles. In my twenty-five years of teaching the personalities, I have never researched how they affect our approach to finances. My husband Fred and I took the money personality test you'll find here and came out as total opposites. While I knew our personalities were opposite of one another, I was surprised to see how different our views of money were. No wonder the many budgets and charts Fred made for me caused me to feel insecure. Charts that seemed simple to Fred were difficult for me.

This book is for all the people in the world who aren't good at financial detail. Rather than being a lofty book on investment strategies, *The Money Makeover* is for real people who don't know how to create a budget and are intimidated by the pale green forms that some seem to use so successfully. But even detail-oriented people, who often experience a clash between their need for perfection and the red marks on their ledger, will find practical advice for getting back on course.

When Rosemarie attended our CLASS seminar for the first time, I was impressed by her energy and enthusiasm. When she came to Advanced CLASS, I had the opportunity to get better acquainted with her. I was amazed at her ability to put concepts that I have difficulty grasping in such a clear and understandable fashion. When I saw her book outline, I encouraged her to get to work and write it. Now here it is for everyone to benefit from.

Well done, Rosemarie. I'm proud of you!

Florence Littauer is the president and founder of CLASS Speakers, Inc., and author of Make the Tough Times Count.

THE MONEY MAKE-OVER

ROSEMARIE F. PATTERSON

First Printing, February 1991

Published by
HERE'S LIFE PUBLISHERS, INC.
P. O. Box 1576
San Bernardino, CA 92402-1576

Printed in the United States of America

Cover illustration by Bruce Day
Cover design by Cornerstone Graphics

Library of Congress Cataloging-in-Publication Data
Patterson, Rosemarie F.
The money makeover : how to get control of your money and your life / Rosemarie F. Patterson.
p. cm.
Includes bibliographical references.
ISBN 0-89840-311-1
1. Finance, personal. 2. Consumer credit. I. Title.
HG179.P295 1990
332.024—dc20 90-21637
CIP

The financial advice in this book is intended for general information purposes only and is not intended as a substitute for personal consultation with qualified financial advisors. Since every reader's personal financial situation is unique, the publisher recommends that readers consult their accountant, financial planner or attorney when implementing any of the information herein.

For More Information, Write:
L.I.F.E.—P.O. Box A399, Sydney South 2000, Australia
Campus Crusade for Christ of Canada—Box 300, Vancouver, B.C., V6C 2X3, Canada
Campus Crusade for Christ—Pearl Assurance House, 4 Temple Row, Birmingham, B2 5HG, England
Lay Institute for Evangelism—P.O. Box 8786, Auckland 3, New Zealand
Campus Crusade for Christ—P.O. Box 240, Raffles City Post Office, Singapore 9117
Great Commission Movement of Nigeria—P.O. Box 500, Jos, Plateau State Nigeria, West Africa
Campus Crusade for Christ International—Arrowhead Springs, San Bernardino, CA 92414, U.S.A.

Contents

Acknowledgments

Without one special person this book surely never would have been written, and to her I owe a debt of love and appreciation. Florence Littauer is a name familiar to millions of people. I feel fortunate to know her and to count her my mentor. It was she who, after seeing my first notes for this book, encouraged me to go forward with it.

Warmest thanks to Dan Benson, my editor, who patiently guided me through several drafts and countless revisions, and never lost his quiet sense of humor and his faith in me, and to Barbara Sherrill, his assistant editor, who shepherded me through all the thorny details.

And lastly, to my husband Pat, who always gives me the courage to put feet on my dreams, and to my family, who put up with me throughout the process. Everlasting love and gratitude.

Before We Begin

Over the years I have counseled many people and, through that process, have been fortunate to learn a good deal about the way people change their spending patterns. The principles which have evolved from that experience are the basis for *The Money Makeover.*

I have a personal distrust of systems of recovery which promise to relieve all our discomfort if we will just follow "these simple rules." However, the entire area of finances often seems so complex and threatening that, in order to emphasize key principles, I have placed them at the beginning of each chapter and called them "steps." I believe anyone can benefit by following these guidelines, although the process can be simple or profound depending upon the depth of insight and hunger for personal freedom that each reader brings to the program.

It is my firm belief that you can change the course of your financial life if you follow these steps. You can be your own debt counselor.

Healing the wounds of financial disease is a process that is sometimes long and painful. Financial success (whatever that means to you) is not a process of learning about arithmetic, or filling out forms. It involves more than devising an intellectual strategy.

To achieve personal financial victory entails emotional as well as spiritual enlightenment. It is an escape to joy as well as freedom. It is my hope that you will find a way to that liberation in these pages.

Rosemarie F. Patterson

1

Getting Control of Your Money and Your Life

Be willing to take effective action for change.

Every happening, great and small, is a parable whereby God speaks to us, and the art of life is to get the message.
—Malcolm Muggeridge

God is not a God of disorder but of peace
(1 Corinthians 14:33, NIV).

Some people never worry about money. How do they do it? They seem to ease through life free from money troubles. They earn the same income as we but live better and worry less. Years ago I thought everybody in the world was organized about money . . . except me.

One of the things I have learned in the past twenty years is that almost everyone is, to some extent, ignorant or disorganized when it comes to money. We don't talk about this, of course. We're afraid to reveal our secret fear that we may be losers when it comes to finances.

It's not a question of brains or education. Even the rich and well-educated sometimes have difficulties. Margaret Truman, bestselling author and daughter of the 33rd president of the United States, once admitted, "I found myself struggling as an adult to balance my chaotic checkbook (lately I've given up)."[1]

For a great many people a balanced budget is just a vague dream. Every year millions of Americans go broke, and nearly one million file bankruptcy.

Is financial disaster something that happens only to Other People? I don't think so. In an uncertain economy, many of us find ourselves asking the searching question, "Where would I be if I were to find myself unemployed for three months?" The answer to that question is, for most of us, "In big trouble." A recent survey indicated that the average working American is just three month's wages—twelve weeks—away from homelessness. In recent years more than 1.3 million Americans had no place to call home, including 100,000 children.

My work as a financial attorney has given me the privilege of helping thousands of people confront their money problems. In talking with individuals who succeeded, I asked, "How did you finally get free of the debt trap?" I felt that if I could study the specific steps they took to turn their lives around, this information could be used to help and encourage others.

In surveying my clients' responses and in reading the life stories of successful men and women, I saw that all of them followed a few simple guidelines. These were principles which anyone could put into practice. I discovered that regardless of education, income or background, everyone can possess financial freedom.

In the chapters that follow I will show you how to put together a financial plan that will fit you, your lifestyle and your personality—and help you fulfill God's plan for your life.

This is not a book about how to get rich. This is not a book about where to put your money to get the most out of your investments. It is not about how to intimidate your way to success in the corporate world. This is just a book about ordinary problems—difficulties that seem so simple you may be ashamed to seek help for them.

What we will do together in the pages of this book is what I like to do for my own clients who come into my office. I am going to pretend that you and I are talking together in person. I will ask you questions, and then I will ask you to take specific actions. Together we will walk through a series of steps that will put you on the road to financial freedom.

Even the Mighty Have Fallen

If you are struggling under a mountain of debt—or buried beneath it—you are in illustrious company. Many prominent men and women have also had money problems. Are any of these names familiar?

Hon. John Connally	Mark Twain
The Hunt Brothers	Harry Truman
Dr. Denton Cooley	Napoleon Bonaparte
Bill Rodgers	Mickey Rooney
Francis Ford Coppola	John DeLorean

These famous people were in serious financial trouble at some time during their lives. But they turned defeat into victory, and you can too.

Before he went on to become the president of the United States, Harry S. Truman spent fifteen years working to recover from the financial reverses of his clothing business that had collapsed in the recession of 1921.

Mark Twain invested in mining and linotype stocks and lost, repeatedly. He was frequently reduced to poverty and hunger as he attempted to subsist on his earnings from writing. If he had struck it rich in his investments, one wonders if he would have persevered with his writing talent to eventually become one of the world's most famous authors.

Napoleon was forced to flee Corsica as his family's estates were confiscated. Before he took command of the

Grand Army of the French Republic he had to burn his household furniture to keep from freezing to death.

The beloved film actor Mickey Rooney has taken a roller-coaster ride from stardom to bankruptcy and back during his lengthy career. In recent years, he has triumphed over financial adversity and made a spiritual and professional comeback at a time of life when many are willing to quit.

These people are super-achievers. They made stunning accomplishments even though they experienced disastrous setbacks along the way. Discouraged many times? Yes. Depressed? You bet. Ashamed, embarrassed beyond words? Undoubtedly. But they reached out for a new beginning. They were not afraid to start again.

Mary Kay Ash, chairman of Mary Kay Cosmetics, Inc., once said, "If you think you can, you can. And if you think you can't, you're right." Nowhere is this more true than in the area of personal finance.

Are You Ready for Action?

The famous people mentioned above had one attribute in common. Without this trait they could not have attained their goals. You, too, must have this quality to reach your aspiration of financial security. What is this characteristic?

It is the willingness to take effective action to bring about change. *Action* is the key word.

Seems simple, doesn't it? Yet, while everyone wants the "good things" of life, most are not willing to do whatever it will take to gain the prize of financial freedom. Action—*effective* action—is necessary for success.

Are you willing to do whatever it takes to win? Are you willing to change your habits, your attitudes, your goals—even your lifestyle—

- to get—and stay—out of debt?
- to have the money you'll need for future emergencies?
- to make some of those "impossible dreams" a reality?
- to be able to give more freely to your church or charity?
- to assure a comfortable retirement?
- to experience the joy of financial freedom?

Without an intense desire to change the course of your life, the Money Makeover will not be of much benefit to you. But if you possess a fervent hunger for financial freedom, you have the characteristic that is the essential key to a new and promising future:

Be willing to take effective action for change.

Martha was a sixty-two-year-old widow who, after a lifetime as a homemaker, was forced to work as a night-shift security guard after the death of her husband. I'll never forget how frightened she appeared at our first interview.

"The creditors are calling, threatening to sue. I don't know what to do." The tears coursed down her cheeks as she probed blindly in her handbag for a tissue.

Here was a woman who had once been attractive and vivacious. Money worries had transformed her into a person fifty pounds overweight, dowdy and depressed. I started leafing through the stack of bills she had handed me. Even without using the calculator, I could see they totaled several thousand dollars.

She swallowed, making a visible attempt to control her trembling voice. "I couldn't keep up with the medical bills during my husband's last illness. Even though we had insurance, it just wasn't enough to cover the treatments. So I started taking cash advances on my credit cards, to pay the rent and buy food." She struggled again to fight back tears.

My heart went out to her. "Martha, it is not going to be easy, but I'll work with you in trying to solve these problems."

I wrote out three rules for her on a sheet of yellow legal paper. (You and I will cover these suggestions, in expanded form, when we get to chapter 4).

"Can you stick to these guidelines for the next three months?" She read the list I handed her and nodded yes.

When she left my office Martha's spirits seemed greatly improved, but as the door closed behind her I wondered about her chances for success. She had so many factors working against her: her age, her lack of job skills, her timidity. How wrong I was!

In the next few months we worked out a repayment plan with her creditors (though not all were cooperative at first). Martha faithfully followed her part of the bargain. She destroyed her credit cards and made small regular payments as arranged. About a year after our first meeting she dropped by the office.

"I know I don't have an appointment, but I had to see you so I could show off a little bit." She stood and performed a slow turn, letting me get the full effect of her stylish lavender knit suit. Knits are not for fatties—and Martha wasn't, not anymore. Her new hairstyle made her look years younger. Even more becoming was her sparkling smile that erased years of worry from her face.

"Martha, you look absolutely marvelous."

As we chatted, she described to me how she had transformed her life.

"Once I started on my money makeover, little by little I started feeling great about myself in other ways. I loved the feeling of control I began to have for the first time in my life. I decided to go on a money diet *and* a reducing diet. I guess I'm one of those people who can be a winner and a loser simultaneously," she quipped.

Today, eight years later, Martha has repaid all her creditors and rebuilt her credit reputation. She has stayed slim *and* out of debt; last year she sent me a note inviting me to her wedding.

I was fortunate to have Martha for a client early in my career. She taught me to not give up on people, because she didn't give up on herself. I have observed many other people who, like Martha, found that the process of getting control of their money had a positive impact on other areas of their lives.

Dr. Judith Rodin, a psychologist at Yale University, says that feelings of control and self-determination are "of central importance in influencing psychological and physical health and perhaps even longevity." The evidence is that lack of control over the direction of our lives can suppress the immune system, rendering our bodies less efficient at fighting off infections and disease.[2] It seems that improving your finances can even improve your health!

Martha was once financially helpless. Now she is living a successful and dynamic life because she was willing to take effective action for change. She learned to take charge of her money, and in so doing, she gained control of her life. You can, too!

I like to tell people about Martha's success because she turned her life around at a time in life when many people start giving up. They begin to believe their lives are almost over and that there is no point in trying to change. They give up on their dreams.

Jenny Guidroz was born in 1932 in the midst of the Depression, the youngest of six children. The family was poor, and Jenny learned early the value of hard work. Her father often worked three jobs while her mother raised chickens and grew vegetables to put food on the table.

After Jenny married she had two daughters and took a part-time job. After the birth of her second daughter, she started putting on weight, so she began working out at a gym. As her interest in physical fitness grew, she went to work for a gym, eventually moving into management.

Though she had never attended college, Jenny refused to let new challenges frighten her. At the age of forty-nine she started a franchise to help people lose weight. At the age of fifty-seven she stated: "It's nice to know if you made mistakes the first half of your life you can spend the second half doing the things that make you happy."

Jenny, the little barefoot Cajun girl, eventually grew up to become known the world over as Jenny Craig, founder of a multi-million dollar international corporation, dedicated to helping others solve their problems with weight control.

Do you believe you have reached a point in life when it is too late to achieve your dreams? Jenny Craig and my friend, Martha, and millions of others who have turned their lives around in mid-stream, exemplify my belief that "it's never too late to take effective action for change."

Money: Love Potion or Poison?

When couples are dating, they enjoy using money to

make their relationship flourish. They exchange gifts and spend money making themselves more attractive to their loved one. At the marriage ceremony they pledge all their emotional and material resources to each other, for life. Yet by the time they reach their first anniversary, they are usually at war about money. Sometimes it is a silent battle for control. The struggle is, however, very real.

Recent studies show that 80 percent of divorces stem from disagreements about money. Psychologists tell us that financial issues are frequently just symptoms of underlying conflict, where money is used as a weapon to control or dominate, instead of as a means of expressing love.

One partner may want to save and spend conservatively, while the other is inclined to squander. When two such opposites are vying for the reins of control, the results can be dynamite. I see many such couples in my practice.

Ed and Lois seemed nervous at our first meeting. As we talked I became aware that they were more than self-conscious—they were profoundly angry with each other. They expressed animosity toward each other in every comment, every glance.

Their immediate problem was that they were facing the loss of their home through foreclosure.

As a result of Ed's layoff from his previous job, they were six months behind in their mortgage payments. Though Ed was now back to work, they were unable to come up with the lump sum of $7,500 in back payments they needed to stop the foreclosure. If we did not act quickly they would lose their home.

Although I recommend bankruptcy protection only as a last resort, it was obvious that Ed and Lois had reached this precipitous point in their finances. I explained that a Chapter 13 bankruptcy would stop the foreclosure and buy them some time to make good on their debts. They could take thirty-six months to catch up on their back house payments. Their credit cards and past-due income taxes could be handled through the plan, without additional interest or penalties. They were delighted and we immediately took steps to file a Chapter 13 petition. The underlying disease, however, could not be cured by this legal protection.

Each time I saw them during the next few months I was struck by the bitterness that seemed almost tangible when the two were together. One day Lois had to stop by the office to sign some documents and I decided to speak up.

"You may not need this information, Lois," I said, "but I'd like you to read over this material and let me know what you think of it." I handed her a pamphlet I had just published titled "Achieving Peace and Prosperity with Your Partner." (You will find this information covered in chapter 11, "When Obstinates Attract.")

I'd like to say that Lois was immediately thrilled that I had singled her out for the honor of reading my thoughts on money/marriage conflicts, but she just glanced at it noncommittally and left without further comment. I felt Ed and Lois's situation was like many others in my practice where anger was the real obstacle to financial security.

Almost twelve months later my hunch was confirmed. The thirty-six months of the Chapter 13 case came to an end, and they received a discharge of their debts. At this point, technically, they were no longer my clients, so I was surprised when they called me for an appointment. We chatted amiably about the weather, their children, and mundane matters for a few moments. I couldn't help noticing all the while that there was something very different about the way they acted toward each other.

"We came to see you because we're in need of some financial advice again, but this time it's because we have good news. We need a bigger house." Ed paused, his proud smile widening. "We're going to have a new baby."

They seemed as cozy as newlyweds.

"I can't believe how lucky I am," Ed said.

"*We* are," Lois corrected him gently.

After I congratulated them, I asked, "What happened? The last time I saw you, I thought you were ready for a divorce."

"Remember that list of things you gave me to do?" Lois reached into a big yellow handbag she had propped next to her chair. She pulled out the pamphlet I had given her almost three years before. "I still carry this around with me. Ed read it too."

Ed was nodding, his arm across the back of his wife's chair, as though unwilling to have even a small unlinked distance between them. "What you said about using money to control other people—that got to me," he said. "I didn't realize that is what I had been doing. It's the way I saw my dad control the family money when we were kids."

Lois was quick to explain her contribution to the problem. "I was afraid of arguments, so I started being sneaky about money. We just couldn't talk about it. When we finally decided to talk openly about our feelings it really made a difference."

If you are one of those people who feels trapped in a relationship with an insensitive, selfish, overspending or penny-pinching mate, there is hope. The Money Makeover is a set of tested guidelines you can start using right away to help strengthen your marriage and your budget. Like Ed and Lois, you can transform your combative marriage into a prosperous partnership—if you are willing to take effective action for change.

Budgets Without Bulges

Any financial plan that is going to work for you over the long haul must be simple to follow. What works for your neighbor might not necessarily work for you or me. Why? Because, for each of us, our approach to money and everything else in life is based upon our personalities.

Charline swooped into my office, flung her fur-trimmed jacket on the chair, and leveled me with a 20-carat amethyst gaze.

"I'm going out of my mind," she blurted, after we had made the preliminary exchanges.

She seemed agitated but far from crazy. I could hardly imagine a more self-contained and in-charge individual. I asked her how I could be of help to her.

She brought her chin up to fighting position but as she did so I could see that it was trembling slightly. "I'm not accustomed to failure. I think I am *reasonably* intelligent. My family is very well-off. But I'm the only one in my family who is disorganized when it comes to money. My sister pays every bill the moment it arrives and even follows the stock market. My father has never had to pay a late charge in his life." She paused to make sure I absorbed the full impact of this information. "And then there is me," she finished tremulously.

She produced a sheaf of overdue bills and presented them to me as though they were something green and slimy. My calculator hummed for a few moments as I tallied up the bad news.

"How would you feel if we could set up a money management system that fits your personality?" I asked her. "One that takes advantage of your strengths without emphasizing your shortcomings?"

She said she was willing to try anything. I gave her a questionnaire and asked her to go home and answer all of the questions. Then, I told her, we would work out a plan that would suit her Money Personality. (In chapters 5 and 6, you and I will talk about *your* Money Personality.)

For the first time, Charline was willing to take effective action for a change in the way she handled her money. Using the strategies you are about to discover, she found a no-guilt system that worked. She was able to solve her problems when she developed a spending program adapted to her unique, creative personality. She sent me a note recently.

> I don't have an IRA yet—maybe next year. And I don't read the *Wall Street Journal,* though I am starting to read the business section of the newspaper. But I don't get those hateful calls from creditors anymore. I can hold my own on money topics, which really makes me feel good about myself. Now that I have my money under control I feel in charge of the rest of my life. I've renewed my financial commitment to my church. I've never felt so productive. I'm not wasting energy trying to be something I'm not. This has given me a peace that was always missing from my life before now.

In *The Money Makeover* we'll find out what type of personality you are and how to utilize your personality strengths to effectively manage your finances. We'll look for ways to build a financial partnership with your spouse, even if he or she is uncooperative. We'll put together a financial strategy that will make use of your unique personality strengths to reach your financial goals.

Need more money?

Want less debt?

In the following pages you will discover how you can accomplish both.

$ $ $

Suggestions for Personal and Group Study

Individuals

The following questions are intended to help you dig deeply into your own heart, to see how ready you are to take specific steps toward change. The answers need not be shared with others unless you wish to do so.

1. How strong is my desire to change the financial direction of my life? Am I willing to make sacrifices to achieve my goals?

2. In the following list, on a scale of 1 to 5, with 1 being "very reluctant" and 5 being "very willing," how willing/reluctant am I to take effective action for change?

   (a) How willing/reluctant am I to set aside time to study about finances? ____

   (b) How willing/reluctant am I to change my attitudes or alter my perceptions if they are proven to be incorrect or harmful to future progress? ____

   (c) Would I be willing/reluctant to "buck the trend," stop going along with the crowd, even stand out as "odd" if I decide I must drastically alter my lifestyle or spending?

   ____

   (d) How willing/reluctant am I to learn about who I really am, accept my limitations, and throw myself with enthusiasm into making the most of my many unique talents? ____

TOTAL SCORE ____

How to score yourself:

1-5 You are too hard on yourself. Re-read chapter 1!

6-10 Why are you letting opinions of others hold you back?

11-15 You can make it, if you stick to your dreams!

16-20 You have the energy it takes to achieve!

Questions for personal reflection:

1. Do I really want to take control of my life, or do I want to passively wait to have other people solve my problems for me?

2. Am I ready to give up blaming my past, my parents, misfortune, and my spouse for my predicament, and get on with the task of building a firm future?

Couples and Groups

After each individual has privately answered the preceding questions, take turns discussing the following.

1. Are we willing to support each other in change? (This is important for couples to consider. If this book is used as a text for group study, it is important that group members pledge utmost confidentiality and emotional support to one another.)

2. Assuming we are willing to support and love each other in change, how will we actively demonstrate to our group or our spouses that they will have our support, our assistance, and our comfort during the growth process?

In words:

In actions:

In commitment to mutual growth:

I, ________________________________, commit my support for change and growth to my group/spouse by words, actions, and self-appraisal and will show my support by the specific steps indicated above.

Date: ___________

Signature: _________________________________

2

Where Does It All Go?

**Step 1:
Make a
written plan.**

*If your outgo exceeds your income,
then your upkeep will be your downfall.*
—Whittier Host Lions Club Bulletin

In my youth I stressed freedom, and in my old age I stress order. I have made the great discovery that liberty is a product of order.
—Will Durant

"Where does it all go?"

I used to ask myself this question before I discovered an amazingly simple system of keeping track of my money. It is simple *to me* because it is geared to my personality and lifestyle. My system might not work for you. Later on in this book I will help you find the strategy that is best for *you*.

Before I knew the secret of monitoring my spending I bought budget books from the drugstore which were full of wonderfully official-looking forms and charts. The trouble was, I could never figure out where veterinary bills, haircuts, paint and plumbing bills fit into the plan. There seemed to be a thousand "miscellaneous" items that were eating away at my salary.

You have probably grappled with your own hit-or-miss method just as I did. You try to make ends meet but there always seem to be more bills than paycheck. You work hard to make more money. Like millions of others you hope that you will eventually arrive at age forty-something with at least a house, a car that is paid for and a few dollars in the bank.

Some years ago I took a look at my list of unfulfilled aspirations and realized it wasn't a list at all—just a hodge-podge of vague hopes. I didn't have my dreams on paper. I didn't have my present circumstances reduced to writing, either.

At that point I decided to start making lists. I made Dream lists, and I made The Way It Is Now lists. I realized that I could not get to any destination unless I knew where I was in the present. Like those maps in shopping malls that say YOU ARE HERE, I had to know where "here" was before I could get to "there."

Don't Be Afraid of the Truth

Most people with money problems hate the thought of picking up a pencil and figuring out what they spend. They are afraid of what they might discover.

A few years ago, a lawyer-friend of mine was diagnosed as having a serious liver ailment. His doctors ordered surgery and then chemotherapy, but after a brief rally, he did not seem to be responding to the course of treatment. Eventually his doctors told him that his illness was terminal and he had less than a year of life remaining.

"Now that you know the truth you can put your remaining time to the very best possible use," his friends tried to comfort him. He would not be consoled. "Until now, I wasted time as though my life would never come to an end. I wish I had never been told how little time I have left."

Some of us are that way about our money. We don't want to know the truth because we will have to confront lost opportunities and poor decisions we have made. Others of us are desperate because we do not believe there is any solution to our problems.

A few days before Christmas in 1988, the *Los Angeles Times* carried an article about a young mother who deliberately plunged her car over a Malibu cliff, killing herself and critically injuring her seven-year-old daughter. The article stated that the woman was despondent about her finances. When I read the story of this pathetic woman and her child, suffering in the midst of a world celebrating the joyous days of Christmas, the faces of many of my clients came to mind.

Thousands of such desperate people have sat in my office and shared their stories with me, letting me into lonely, hidden corners of their lives. Some are so depressed that they have lost their ability to manage their daily affairs. They are sure they are utter failures. They are starting to believe that life is just not worth the struggle. Their disease? Financial despair.

Perhaps you too have felt helpless, hopeless, ashamed and alone because you cannot pay your bills. If you are living this kind of pain, first let me tell you that I have also walked along that road, and so have many others. Part of the hurt comes from a false belief that you are the only one stupid enough to have made these kinds of mistakes. The rest comes from not knowing what to do about your mistakes, or believing that there is nothing that can be done to change your situation.

In the following chapters we will work together to deal with those two areas: (a) We will help you gather information from your own experience that is useable to you, and supportive of who you are; and (b) We will help you take effective action in your own finances.

What can you do to ensure your progress? First, I will ask you to read through the book carefully, chapter by chapter. Parts of it may seem especially interesting to you, while others may seem dull and boring. Stick with the tedious parts, as well as the fun parts, won't you? Work the exercises at the end of each chapter. If possible, enlist the aid of a study group. Let others give you encouragement and provide a structure of accountability to your peers. It works.

Action is a vital part of this program. *Reading* about change and *thinking* about change and *talking* about change won't bring about change. Action—new behaviors—help bring about change. By doing the "homework assignments" in each chapter, you will be actively bringing about your own recovery.

A very real component of financial failure is the numbing depression that accompanies it. Every time you start to feel low about your finances, you can look at your goal worksheets and your decision lists, and your progress will lift you.

Why a "Standard" Budget Doesn't Work

Years ago, before I met and married my husband Pat, I was a young divorced mother and sole support of three little girls. There was no one to whom I could go and say, "Look—here's my paycheck, and here is a list of my living expenses. Help me figure out what to do."

I had no idea how to manage the little bit of money I earned. I had grown up in a home where there was never any money to manage. We didn't have a checking account or an automobile. We were just happy to get by. When I got out on my own I had to learn from scratch. True to my nature and background, I was disorganized about keeping track of details.

I looked for answers in the public library. There I found handbooks on how to make wise investments, volumes on how to strike it rich in real estate, and manuals with charts and budgets, none of which addressed my needs.

Finally I devised my own system. Years later when I became a financial attorney, I discovered to my surprise that the simple methods I had used also worked for my clients who (like me) were allergic to forms, hated bookkeeping, and loathed the very sound of the word "budget."

Vernon Law, who pitched for the Pittsburgh Pirates, once said, "Experience is a hard teacher because she gives the test first, the lesson afterward."[1] I passed my financial test the hard way, and years later I discovered why my system worked. It worked because it fit me, fit my lifestyle, and fit my personality. And it worked because I made it work.

These guidelines are simple but they are not automatic, and not all of them are easy. They will take effort. Some of them will take practice and may even require—ugh!—some *discipline.* Follow along with me as we work together, one principle at a time, to find the solutions to your special problems. But first, let's examine the first step to financial success.

Step 1:
Make a written plan.

After a few years in law practice, I stumbled on an astonishing discovery. Not one of the people who came to me seeking bankruptcy relief had a complete, written spending plan.

In other words, a budget.

Not one!

Can you, right now, answer the following questions with absolute certainty?

1. How much after-tax, spendable income do you have each month?

2. What do you spend each month on basic living expenses such as mortgage or rent, food, utilities, clothing?

3. What is the total amount of money you owe to all creditors?

4. What are your specific financial goals for the next five years?

Don't despair if you do not have accurate responses right at the tip of your tongue. That just means you're like most people! But, as I've already pointed out, most people have financial problems, and you have already made up your mind that you are going to be different. You are going to be financially free.

Gina and Fred—Facing Facts

When they came in for their first appointment, Gina and Fred couldn't tell me their exact monthly spendable income. They didn't know how much they owed their creditors. And they had absolutely no idea what they wanted to achieve in five years, financially or otherwise.

Like a lot of people they were so busy raising their three children that they had never set aside the time to analyze their money situation. They managed their finances the way most of us do, by instinct and impulse.

Some of their money habits had been formed in childhood. Their parents had lived from paycheck to paycheck, without hope of a brighter financial future. Gina and Fred had adopted the same attitudes. They had no idea how to set up a spending plan. They had no idea how powerful a written five-year plan could be. After years of struggling, they were deeply in debt, behind in their rent, and facing bankruptcy.

Instead of focusing on their failures, I asked them about their hopes. "Tell me a little bit about your dreams for the future," I said.

The question seemed to startle them at first, as though this were not the sort of question they were entitled to consider. Then, a bit shyly, Gina began to open up. "We'd like to have our own house someday. In a nice neighborhood, away from the gangs."

"I'd maybe like to have my own car repair business," Fred added softly.

"He's a good mechanic—he can fix anything," Gina added proudly.

"Let's write those things down on a list," I said. I pulled a sheet from a yellow legal pad and wrote, *Five-Year Plan*. "On another sheet of paper, let's make a list of your bills. During this next week I'd like you to figure out how much you are paying your creditors in interest charges every year. Fill out this questionnaire too, so you can see how you are spending your money. Will you do that?" They agreed, and we made an appointment for the next Friday.

A week later Fred was not the same sullen, hopeless man I had first encountered. He seemed ready to burst with energy. He'd made an important discovery that would change his financial life, and he couldn't wait to share his news. "I can't believe how much we pay out in interest! If we could just pay cash for everything we could save more than $3,000 every year."

"With that amount of money, we could buy a good car in three years and pay cash," Gina said wistfully. "Or have a down payment for a house."

"The trouble is, we're so far in debt I can't see how we can ever get on a cash program."

"That's the next step," I explained. "First, find out how you're spending. Then decide where to make adjustments."

Armed with a set of Money Makeover Decision Lists, they left my office with a look of new determination. In the following weeks Fred and Gina made up a list of temporary cutbacks which would start them toward their goal of being debt-free. I gave them a few suggestions, but they provided the necessary underpinnings of what was to become, for them, a successful financial reorganization plan. How were they able to do this?

They made a written plan.

The Three-Legged Stool

The Money Makeover Spending Plan is like a three-legged stool. If one leg gets too long, the stool topples over. They have to be in balance with each other in order to support your goals.

What are these three "legs"? They are three promises I am going to ask you to make to yourself. They are all equally important. In your Money Makeover, you will be promising yourself:

- to spend joyfully
- to spend practically
- to spend securely

Do you have a commitment to use your money in ways that will produce long-lasting joy for yourself, for others, and for God? That commitment is going to express itself in the way you give, spend and save.

Are you willing to promise to spend in ways that will ensure present, practical benefits? That commitment is going to affect the physical environment in which you live.

And, lastly, will you promise to plan for long-term security and stability in your financial dealings? That commitment is going to impact your future, and the lives of those who depend upon you.

These are the three foundations of the balanced spending plan. Within the framework of these commitments, as you will see, there is almost infinite room to express your own goals and personality. It is possible to have a budget that works and one that meets your deepest needs for joy, practicality, and security. In the following pages I will show you how.

Joy: The Heart of Your Spending Plan

James Thurber is quoted as saying, "Laughter need not be cut out of anything, since it improves everything."[2]

Nowhere is laughter—happiness—more essential than in your budget. The Bible tells us, "A joyful heart is good medicine" (Proverbs 17:22, NASB). And "Do not be grieved, for the joy of the Lord is your strength" (Nehemiah 8:10, NASB). Joy is a sign of emotional health. It is a worshipful way in which our spiritual natures can shout a "Yes!" to God. So we are going to deliberately build joy into your spending plan.

Many people put practical necessities at the top of their budgets. Sometimes budgets are so full of practicalities that they never get beyond that into the realm of emotional needs. But we are creatures of desire, emotion, longings. So it is important that JOY be given importance in the spending plan.

The Practical Commitment

Tom and Kate took a lavish European vacation, but were evicted from their apartment a few months later. They had been spending all their money on fun things and had neglected their practical needs. A friend of mine spent her whole paycheck on a new fall wardrobe and couldn't pay her light bill. Has anything like this ever happened to you?

If so, you are like many of us. But there is a way to overcome that urge to splurge.

The rewards of a commitment to a practical lifestyle are many. When these needs are met, we have a pleasing environment, well-maintained belongings, and an existence that feels orderly and satisfying. We can face the day with confidence knowing we have taken care of the physical business of living.

The Secure Lifestyle

A good spending plan provides for future needs as well as daily necessities and happiness. It should cushion us from the hard realities of life such as illness, old age, inflation and unemployment. It prepares us for car breakdowns and roof repairs.

The Money Makeover will help you to plan for rain while you are enjoying the sunshine. Your family's sense of unity and direction are greatly affected by attention to longterm stability. Children who grow up in homes where parents focus on deeper, permanent fulfillment have a healthy confidence. They have stability. Children need this to face the challenges of growing up.

Joyful, Practical and Secure: the three legs of the Money Makeover Spending Plan. Three promises you will make to spend joyfully, spend practically and spend securely.

In chapter 4, you will be asked a number of questions about the ways you are now using money. With this information you can begin preparing your own Money Makeover.

But before we do that, in the next chapter I am going to show you how to accomplish one of the most important steps you must take to achieve financial success.

$ $ $

Suggestions for Personal and Group Study

Individuals

1. What is Step 1 for personal growth in financial freedom?

2. Is discouragement over money problems robbing you of the energy you need to make a fresh start?

   Study the following Scriptures:

   1 Peter 5:7
   Exodus 33:14
   Isaiah 41:10
   Matthew 7:7,8
   Psalm 112:7
   Psalm 34:17
   Matthew 11:28
   Psalm 91:4

3. Inaction and indecision produce feelings of helplessness, confusion and depression. Here are the positive steps you can take right now to lift the weight of discouragement.

   - Continue reading and studying this book.
   - Make a list of benefits you will achieve by applying these principles.
   - Make a dream list.
   - Pray and ask for God's love to surround you.
   - Memorize the Scripture verses listed under question 2 above.

4. Review the four questions we asked about your present financial situation (page 32). Do you have this information at hand?

5. To what extent have you been unwilling in the past to face the truth about your financial situation? Why? Are you afraid that confronting the truth will create problems in your marriage? To your self-esteem? Will the truth force you to make decisions or changes which presently seem frightening?

6. What part, if any, has simple laziness played in your apathy or depression? Is this laziness/helplessness/apathy related to lack of hope?

Group Discussion

1. Is there a a difference between joy and happiness? Explain your answer.

2. In what ways do you think joy can be incorporated into a financial plan?

3. In what ways is joy missing from your present financial plan?

4. What keeps us from expressing joy in our finances? Worry, guilt, greed, lack of sufficient income, too many debts? Why?

5. List obstacles to joy below, to be reviewed for later discussion and problem-solving.

6. Joy can be defined as a spiritual shout of "Yes!" to God. In what other ways might joy be defined or expressed?

3

Getting Organized for Success

Step 2: Make a Budget Box.

Most ignorance is vincible ignorance.
We don't know because we don't want to know.
—Aldous Huxley

When you enjoy becoming wise, there is hope for you!
A bright future lies ahead!
(Proverbs 24:14, TLB)

"Turn that television off right now and come dry the dishes."

Somewhere in America, a mother is saying that to a teenager. And from the living room a little voice replies dreamily, "Just a minute, Mom."

Just a minute. Do you ever hear that expression in your home? I heard it with my teenagers, and I'll bet you've heard it too.

Just a minute. It's the theme song of the procrastinator. My kids probably picked up both the melody and the lyrics from me—I am one of the world's champion procrastinators.

I would much rather daydream, plan, make lists and talk about doing something than actually get right down to the nitty-gritty of doing it. Most of my clients—those who have money problems—also suffer from this malaise.

I am told that there is a fellow somewhere in Iowa

who has been meaning to start a Procrastinators Club but he hasn't gotten around to it yet. I'm going to assume you're like me and like most of the people I counsel. I'm going to take it for granted you're one of us, a charter member of Procrastinators Anonymous, but one who has been missing a lot of meetings lately. Welcome to the club.

It won't do you any good to read about other people's successes until you dig in and start getting your own success story started. Remember, you must be willing to take effective action for change. *Action* is the operative word. Don't wait until you have read this entire book.

We are at the point where I am going to ask you to take your first important action step. This one bit of homework will cost you about an hour of time and a few dollars, but will pay great dividends.

Step 2:
Make a Budget Box.

In a minute I'll show you how to do this. But first I want you to savor a few of the benefits. The rewards of owning and maintaining a Budget Box are almost endless. You will save hundreds of hours that you now waste looking for lost papers. Remember the time the toaster broke down two weeks after you bought it, and you couldn't locate the warranty? Remember the time the lights were turned off because you misplaced the bill?

A Budget Box will give you confidence, order and peace of mind. These are priceless commodities.

Assembling Your Budget Box

If you are serious about getting your money under

control, you must find and stick to a simple system of keeping your records.

If you're like me, this could mean that you will have to give up that most treasured of family traditions: the kitchen junk drawer. I confess that as a young woman, I always had a kitchen junk drawer. I can now say that after lengthy rehabilitation on the Makeover system, I am now completely *drawer-free!* Even after years of such sober living, however, I still get slightly nostalgic when I think about some of my favorite junk drawers.

A really good junk drawer contains: old report cards, bills (opened and unopened), the 1980 census survey you forgot to turn in, Disneyland "A" tickets from 1978, broken rubber bands, screws and other metal parts that you're afraid to throw away because as soon as you do you'll need them, hair pins, trash bag ties, bottle openers, old shopping lists, receipts, manufacturer's instructions for the toaster you threw out last year, four rolls of undeveloped film that are at least two years old, and Mother's Day cards that are so sweet you can't bear to throw them away.

Believe me, I appreciate the sanctity of the kitchen junk drawer.

I once had a neighbor who surpassed me. She not only had a junk drawer in her kitchen that defied all description for variety and antiquity of contents, she also had a whole room devoted to junk. Into it she literally threw all the ironing she had not done. (In those days, we owned ironing boards and actually ironed pillow cases. Now you don't need to ask me how old I am. You know.) Any time anyone left anything lying around for more than a minute the door to the junk room was opened, and—*woosh*!—the offending item disappeared. I always thought it would be a great place to hide the old newspapers my husband likes to keep, but I never had a whole room I could spare for that purpose.

I think you will agree, if you think about it for a moment, that a Budget Box is infinitely superior to a kitchen junk drawer or even a junk room.

Don't make it complicated.

You don't need an office, or a whole desk, or even a file cabinet. Just a sturdy cardboard box from the stationery store will do—the kind offices use to store old files.

Stock your Budget Box with a set of A-Z file folders. These will be used to hold correspondence and receipts that do not fit into the specialized folders that I will tell you about next. Add five or six plain folders that you can label: *Bills to Pay*, *Taxes*, *Health*, *Utilities*, etc. You can file all your different types of insurance in one folder or in separate folders.

I like to group related categories in one single file folder. I buy the heavy pressboard file folders which have six separate divisions within them; they are available at most stationery stores. One such folder is labeled *Auto.* Inside are separate sections labeled *Insurance*, *Repairs*, *Registration*, *Auto Savings*. By going to just one folder, I can find all the paperwork and bills related to the cars. I keep separate folders for each car so I can see how much each costs to operate.

I keep the same type of folder for utilities. Instead of filing bills for electricity, gas, and water in separate folders, I have one heavy-duty folder marked *Utilities.* Within this folder are separate sections labeled *Water*, *Electricity*, *Cable Television*, *Gas*, and so forth.

Into your Budget Box will go a lot of papers that are now hiding in your kitchen junk drawer and gathering dust on the top of the refrigerator. Remember all those instruction books and warranty cards for your household appliances? File them under *A* for *Appliances* or *W* for *Warranties and Instructions*, or whatever works for you.

Into the Budget Box will also go the category envelopes which we will discuss in chapter 8. In the alphabetical folders you can keep receipts for cash purchases.

Our box has a large expansion-type folder, open on top, which is labeled *Bills to Pay*. The Budget Box is kept in the kitchen where it is always accessible. When a bill arrives in the mail it is placed in the Budget Box, until it is time to write checks. No more lost bills.

In the Budget Box there is a large, professional-type checkbook that never leaves the house. (More about this later.)

I keep a lidded plastic container (the kind used to store leftovers) in my Budget Box to store such things as stamps, envelopes, paper clips, pens, pencils, rubber bands, and a small stapler. Nothing is more annoying than to discover that it is time to pay a bill and you don't have stamps or envelopes! This is where I store a small solar-powered calculator that I enjoy because it never needs paper, re-inking or an electric outlet. This means I can take my Budget Box out to the patio on nice afternoons and do my financial work under the trees.

It is so convenient to have a fully-contained, portable Budget Box, complete with checkbook, bills, calculator, and supplies, which I can carry with me anywhere. Once we went to the beach for a weekend and I wanted to work on our budget, so I just put the Budget Box into the back of the station wagon with our luggage, and away we went. Pat and I were still able to squeeze in our financial planning session while enjoying our getaway. We are not always this disciplined, but sometimes we like to surpass ourselves.

The Complete Budget Box

The complete Budget Box contains:

- A-Z folders
- Open top, expansion-type file folder labeled *Bills to Pay*
- Heavy-duty, multi-section folders labeled:
    - *Utilities* (*Gas, Electric, Cable, Water*)
    - *Auto* (*Insurance, Registration, #1 Car Repairs, #2 Car Repairs*)
    - *House* (*Insurance, Payments, Homestead, Deed, Lease, Repairs, Improvements*)
    - *Credit Cards* (*Mastercard, Visa,* etc.)
- Plastic container with lid for: clips, pens, postage stamps, envelopes, solar-powered calculator
- Checkbook: large, professional-size

Does this sound complicated? It's not. It will take you one trip to the stationery store and post office, and about one hour to set it up. The investment in time and money will do wonders for your ego. The entire cost, including a full roll of first-class stamps, should be less than $40.

You don't have any excuse whatever not to have a place to keep your bills and records. None. You have a place for less important things, don't you? You even have a place for your trash—a waste basket. You wouldn't throw your trash on the floor or leave it lying around. It's odd that we can be disciplined about where we put our trash but lazy about where we keep our bills and important records.

When clients come to me for financial counseling one of the first things I ask them is whether they have a place where they keep all their records in order. When the answer is no, which it usually is, I tell them to go out and get a box like the one described above. When they schedule their next appointment, I ask them to bring their Budget Box with them. If they don't have one yet, I tell them I can't help them with a financial plan until they do.

If you keep postponing the job of putting together your Budget Box, you should ask yourself why. Are you deliberately trying to conceal the truth from yourself? Is it because you know that, once you get organized, you will be confronted with the facts, and that may require you to make changes? Believe me, reality can't possibly hurt you more than living in a fog of ignorance.

If you don't have a Budget Box, don't put it off. Get it together today.

$ $ $

Suggestions for Personal and Group Study

Individuals

1. Have you put together your Budget Box yet? If not, why not?

2. If you do not have a Budget Box, do you have an alternative organization process? Analyze it to see if it meets the following guidelines:

   a. You have all bills and receipts filed in one location and in order so they can be easily located.

b. You can quickly tell how much you owe on every obligation.

c. You have your tax records organized for easy retrieval of this information at the end of the year.

d. You have all the family's medical records, vaccination dates, etc., in one easy-to-find location in case of emergency.

3. If your bills and records are not fully organized, set a deadline one week from today, and get started! Each day work a little bit on the project, breaking it up into manageable tasks. This is the most important first step you can take!

Groups

Note to Group Leader: The process of getting physically organized is absolutely essential to the Money Makeover. Don't let the group slight this important first step toward financial freedom. It may take several weeks before some members complete the process, but keep following up with them and reminding them that this is essential to success. Possibilities for group discussion or activities:

1. Have members of the group bring their Budget Boxes and demonstrate any shortcuts or tips they may have discovered during the process of getting organized.

2. Some people have found they like to decorate the boxes with wallpaper, paint or glued-on fabric.

3. In the ensuing weeks, encourage members to continue to bring in their boxes and work together as a group on labeling, listing, filing and so forth.

4. Have members discuss problems they encountered and share solutions.

5. Ask members to share positive aspects of getting organized. Ask open-ended questions such as, "How does the process of getting organized add to your feeling of self-esteem (or control or optimism)?"

6. Have members of the group report to each other, setting deadlines for those who are procrastinating, offering encouragement and support.

4

Know Where Your Money Goes

Step 3: Complete the Money Makeover Inventory.

The secret of success is constancy to purpose.
—Benjamin Disraeli

And let us not get tired of doing what is right,
for after a while we will reap a harvest of blessing
if we don't get discouraged and give up
(Galatians 6:9, TLB).

Most people have some sort of rough monthly budget. Sometimes it is just a set of figures they carry around in their heads: Rent, Food, Car Payment, and of course, that lovely catch-all, Miscellaneous.

The trouble with this kind of budget is that it is grossly inaccurate. How can a budget with only eight items be accurate? It does not include things like Thanksgiving, Christmas, anniversaries, house guests, broken washing machines, vet bills, Girl Scout cookies and a thousand-and-one other things that eat at the paycheck. Most "monthly budgets" actually underestimate living expenses by 35 percent or more.

The Miscellaneous Muddle

Most budget books have a catch-all category that includes everything from Christmas presents and political donations to raffle tickets and family photos. What is this classification that is the hands-down favorite spending division? *Miscellaneous.* It is the area that causes the most trouble and confusion.

Miscellaneous is the fun stuff. If you had no Miscellaneous in your life you might not buy your dog his license, never celebrate your wedding anniversary, get a haircut or rent a video movie.

For most of us, Miscellaneous is the "style" in "lifestyle."

Miscellaneous can be grand, gaudy and garish. But for the rest of us, Miscellaneous is the money that makes our daily lives work, the oil that lubricates the "life machine." It is the money we spend making ourselves and others a little bit more *happy.*

When I started writing out a spending plan for myself, I discovered that Miscellaneous was devouring approximately 35 percent of my income. Because I could not get a grip on it, Miscellaneous was destroying my budget. I realized there was only one way to get control of my money and my life. I had to get rid of my Miscellaneous.

The Money Makeover Inventory will help you do this—and much more! It will help you put a microscope to your budget. You will have a complete financial profile. You will know what your credit card purchases are really costing you. You will know how much it costs to operate your car.

You've probably heard the expression, "Garbage In, Garbage Out," a computer maxim that means our results can be no better than the quality of the input. Before your brain can produce sensible financial decisions you must have high-quality information.

The Money Makeover Inventory is designed to help you get that data.

Typical Budget Snares

Automobiles

Many people list gasoline costs under "Transportation," and count the monthly car payment plus gasoline and oil as the total cost of the car. However, in order to find out the truth about your transportation costs, you should include all expenses associated with the vehicle. Car insurance should be included as part of the cost of your car, not as "Insurance" or "Miscellaneous." Auto maintenance, gasoline, depreciation and insurance all have to do with total operating costs. Separate the costs for each car. In this way you can compare the cost of driving a particular automobile with alternative modes of transportation or another model of automobile.

Write down your odometer reading for each car at the beginning of the month or when you fill the gas tank so you can see how many miles you are driving. It costs approximately $.30 per mile to drive an automobile, when you include wear on tires, repairs, insurance and maintenance. Depending on the type of automobile, this figure may or may not include depreciation. Take a hard look at the miles you drive and consider if they can be reduced. Should you car pool? Take public transportation? Drive a more economical type of car? Cut out unnecessary trips or aimless "Sunday drives"?

All of these questions will start to present themselves when you know your monthly (and yearly) mileage totals and consider how much it costs to drive each mile.

Food

Your check to the grocer might easily include a lawn rake, baby bottles, diapers, cosmetics, soft drinks, chewing gum, and a host of other non-food items. If you are going to plug your money leaks it is essential that you separate real food from all the non-food items. I know this is difficult.

My husband Pat and I found a solution that works for us. We go shopping together. This adds a certain balance to our purchases, and has turned out to be a good time to broaden our perspectives about "where all the money goes." Each of us takes a separate shopping cart and a separate shopping list. All non-food items—anything that can't be strictly regarded as food—goes into Pat's basket. All the ordinary food products go into my basket. At the checkout stand, we make out two separate checks—one for the non-food products, another for the groceries.

This system has enabled us to keep track of what we spend for food. We can also see how much is spent for cleaning supplies, batteries, and other items which could be purchased for less at a discount or department store.

Housing

Most budget guides list rent or mortgage payments separately from all of the other expenses which go with housing. We look at our budgets and see the monthly mortgage payment listed there, and we tend to think that is what it costs to own the house. That's why some budgets actually foster misconceptions about where the money is going.

The Money Makeover Inventory brings together the costs of fertilizer, plumbing repair, paint and sprinklers, as well as the multitudes of sneaky items such as linens, furnishings, household help, and appliance repairs. All of these should be viewed together as total Housing Costs.

The annual maintenance costs of a home average from 2 percent to 3 percent of the house's fair market value, including carpets, paint, furniture depreciation and so forth. That means that a $100,000 house will cost from $2,000 to $3,000 annually. These figures vary, obviously, based upon your ability to make ordinary household repairs and your cleverness in finding bargains. No matter how resourceful you may be, though, the furnace is not immortal. It will deteriorate.

My son-in-law Jeff, who is an engineer/lawyer, tells me this is the Law of Entropy. Jeff is a genius and likes to organize information into neatly labeled modules. It's probably from all those years he spent in school. This combination of legal and scientific training is probably not good for kids. Because of it, Jeff likes to feel that laws permeate every aspect of daily life. He is a nice son-in-law, so we don't argue with him about this.

Whether it is entropy or not, your house and everything in it is wearing out, not just on paper, but in reality. (Accountants don't call this entropy; they call it depreciation.) You may put off roof repairs for a number of years but eventually it will need costly attention. Come to think of it, even my son-in-law will eventually wear out, though it hasn't started to show yet.

Fair Market Values: What They Mean to Your Budget

On the Money Makeover Inventory you will list the present fair market value of such things as your home and automobiles. You need to know the fair market value of the things you own. Let's say that the car you bought brand new eight months ago now has a Blue Book value of 60 percent of its purchase price. Isn't this important information when you are planning for your next car?

If you need a bigger house, and are thinking of selling the one you now own, you need to know what you would net *after costs of sale.* This will help you to compare the advantages of moving compared to building an addition to your present home, for example.

You should be aware of the rate of interest you are paying to use credit, and what that means to you in actual dollars every month.

When you approach the sections on the Joyful Lifestyle Commitment, many of your figures may be rough estimates. Is it a waste of time to guess at what you spend? I think not. Even though you have not been keeping accurate records, when you sit down with a pencil and paper you will be surprised how you will be able to restructure from memory the way you customarily spend.

The Unplanned Essentials

Some of my clients come to me seriously worried because they have no health insurance or car insurance. Perhaps they know that they should be getting regular dental checkups, but they haven't been able to afford proper treatment.

Even if you have not been buying insurance or getting medical checkups, good stewardship (and in many instances, the law) requires that you provide for these necessities. I want you to list these items on your Inventory and put a star next to them. Later on you can gradually integrate these asterisked items in your spending plan one by one by cutting spending in less important categories.

Are you ready to go?

Step 3:
Complete the Money Makeover Inventory.

Take time to answer the questions as fully as you can. Believe me, the time you spend will be repaid many times over.

THE MONEY MAKEOVER INVENTORY

THE JOYFUL LIFESTYLE COMMITMENT

Donations and Giving

1. Monthly tithe $ ____
2. Monthly giving over and above tithes $ ____
3. Other ______________________ $ ____
______________________ $ ____
______________________ $ ____

MONTHLY TOTAL: **$ ____**

Multiply by 12. ANNUAL TOTAL: **$ ____**

(Copy monthly total to line 1 on page 75.)

I/We commit to give the following in non-monetary gifts:

Recipient	Gift
______________________	______________
______________________	______________
______________________	______________

*In the future I/we hope to set aside $ ____ per month ($ ____ per year) in addition to foregoing, for giving to ______________________.

Personal Gift Giving

1. Make a list of family members, friends and business associates for whom you buy gifts throughout the year. In the columns at the right, estimate the approximate amount you spend for each gift.

Name	Amount Spent For: Birthday	Anniversary	Holidays
Totals:	$ ____ Birthdays	$ ____ Anniversaries	$ ____ Holidays

ANNUAL TOTAL (total of all 3 columns): $ ____

Divide by 12. MONTHLY TOTAL: $ ____

(Copy monthly total to line 2 on page 75.)

*In the future I/we want to set aside $ ________ per month ($ _____ per year) in addition to the foregoing for the purpose of ________________________________.

Recreation, Entertainment, Vacations

1. a. How many times a month do you eat out, including work lunches? _____
   b. How much do you spend each time, including tip? $ _____
   c. How much do you spend each time on a babysitter? $ _____
   d. Add together (b) and (c) and multiply by (a). Monthly Total: $ _____
   e. Multiply (d) by 12. Annual Total: $ _____

2. a. How many times per month do you bowl, play tennis, golf, ski, skate, attend ball games? ____
   b. How much do you spend each time? $ ____
   c. How much do you spend each time for a sitter? $ ____
   d. What do you spend on parking, food, or incidentals each time? $ ____
   e. Add together (b), (c) and (d), and multiply by (a). Monthly Total: $ ____
   f. Multiply (e) by 12. Annual Total: $ ____

3. a. How many times per year do you take short vacation trips to the river, mountains, beach or desert? ____
   b. How much do you spend each time? $ ____
   c. What do you spend on babysitters, equipment rentals, parking or incidentals each time? $ ____
   d. Add together (b), (c), and multiply by (a). Annual Total: $ ____
   e. Divide (d) by 12. Monthly Total: $ ____

4. a. How many times per month do you entertain friends or relatives in your home? ____
   b. How much do you spend for food, beverages, each time? $ ____
   c. Multiply (a) times (b). Monthly Total: $ ____
   d. Multiply (c) by 12. Annual Total: $ ____

5. a. How many times per year do you host friends or relatives for special holidays, such as Thanksgiving, Christmas? ____
   b. How much do you spend on food, beverages for each occasion? $ ____

c. How much for home decorations, flowers, clothing? $ ____

d. Add together (b) and (c).
Annual Total: $ ____

e. Divide (d) by 12. Monthly Total: $ ____

6. a. What do you spend on annual vacations?
Annual Total: $ ____

b. Divide (a) by 12. Monthly Total: $ ____

TOTAL OF ITEMS 1 - 6
MONTHLY TOTAL: $ ____
ANNUAL TOTAL: $ ____

(Copy monthly total to line 3 on page 75.)

*In the future I/we want to set aside $ ________ per month ($ ____ per year) in addition to the foregoing for the purpose of ______________________________.

Health, Beauty and Self-Improvement

1. a. How many times a year do members of your family get haircuts? ____

b. How much do you spend for each haircut?
$ ____

c. Multiply (a) times (b). Annual Total: $ ____

2. How much is spent annually for:

a. Permanents $ ____

b Manicures $ ____

c. Gym or Spa Membership $ ____

d. Cosmetics $ ____

e. Shaving cream, aftershave, etc. $ ____

f. Other $ ____

3. a. How much is spent for lessons, such as a musical instrument, dance, voice, annually? $ ____

   b. Other ______________________ $ ____

ANNUAL TOTAL: **$ ____**

Divide by 12. MONTHLY TOTAL: **$ ____**

(Copy monthly total to line 4 on page 75.)

*In the future I/we want to set aside $ _______ per month ($ _____ per year) in addition to the foregoing for the purpose of ______________________________.

Animals and Pets

1. Pet food (amount spent each week x 52 =) $ ____
2. Annual veterinarian bills, checkups, shots $ ____
3. Pet boarding care (during vacations, trips) annually $ ____
4. Training or other, annually $ ____

ANNUAL TOTAL: **$ ____**

Divide by 12. MONTHLY TOTAL: **$ ____**

(Copy monthly total to line 5 on page 75.)

*In the future I/we want to set aside $ ________ per month ($ _____ per year) in addition to the foregoing for the purpose of ______________________________

THE PRACTICAL LIFESTYLE COMMITMENT

Housing Payments

1. Monthly house payment or rent:

1st Trust Deed/Creditor Name

____

Total balance $ _____

Monthly payment $ _____

Is the note fully amortized or is there a "balloon payment"? If yes, when is it due? _____

Annual amount applied to principal reduction $ _____

Annual amount applied to interest $ _____

2nd Trust Deed/Creditor Name

____

Total balance $ _____

Monthly payment $ _____

Is the note fully amortized, or is there a "balloon payment"? If yes, when is it due? _____

Annual amount applied to principal reduction $ _____

Annual amount applied to interest $ _____

3rd Trust Deed/Creditor Name

____

Total balance $ _____

Monthly payment $ _____

Is the note fully amortized, or is there a "balloon payment"? If yes, when is it due? _____

Annual amount applied to principal reduction $ ____

Annual amount applied to interest $ ____

Monthly House Payment/Rent Total $ ____

Multiply by 12. Annual House Payment/Rent Total $ ____

Copy monthly and annual totals to Housing Costs recap on page 65.

2. a. Homeowner Insurance, annually $ ____

   b. Divide 2a by 12.
      Homeowner Insurance, monthly $ ____

Copy annual and monthly totals to Housing Costs recap on page 63.

3. a. Property taxes, annually $____

   b. Divide 3a by 12.
      Property taxes, monthly $ ____

Copy annual and monthly totals to Housing Costs recap on page 65.

*In the future I/we want to set aside $ _______ per month ($ _____ per year) in addition to the foregoing for the purpose of ________________________________.

Utilities

Go back over your checkbook or old receipts. Add up six months of expenses in each of the following categories, and divide by six. What is the average amount you spend monthly on:

Gas $ ____

Electric $ ____

Water $ ____
Telephone $ ____
Trash $ ____
Cable TV $ ____

MONTHLY TOTAL $ ____

Multiply by 12. ANNUAL TOTAL $ ____

Copy monthly and annual totals to Housing Costs recap on page 65.

*In the future I/we want to set aside $ _______ per month ($ _____ per year) in addition to the foregoing for the purpose of ______________________________.

Home Maintenance and Repairs

List below the approximate amount you spend annually for the following items. Note: As a general rule, home maintenance and repairs, including replacement of furniture and incidentals, amounts to an average of 2 to 3 percent of the market value of your home each year. Some years you will spend less, others more, but you should have an amount planned for this item.

1. Interior Maintenance and Repairs
   a. Carpet and drapery cleaning $ ____
   b. Appliance repair $ ____
   c. Painting, interior $ ____
   d. Furniture replacement $ ____
   e. Housekeeping $ ____
   f. Other ____________________ $ ____
2. Exterior Maintenance and Repair
   a. Roof repair and replacement $ ____

b. Walkways, driveways $ ____
c. Rain gutters, fireplace cleaning, etc. $ ____
d. Termite and pest control $ ____

3. Gardening and Landscaping

a. Plants, trees and seeds $ ____
b. Fertilizer and sprays $ ____
c. Sprinkler installation and repairs $ ____
d. Pool chemicals $ ____
e. Pool cleaning service $ ____
f. Gardening service $ ____
g. Other ________________________ $ ____

ANNUAL TOTAL: **$ ____**

Divide by 12. MONTHLY TOTAL: **$ ____**

Copy annual and monthly totals to Housing Costs recap below.

*In the future I/we want to set aside $ _______ per month ($ _____ per year) in addition to the foregoing for the purpose of ________________________________.

Housing Costs Recap

	Monthly	Annually
Payments	______	______
Insurance	______	______
Property Taxes	______	______
Total All Utilities	______	______
Maintenance, Repairs	______	______
TOTAL all housing costs:	______	______

(Copy monthly total of all housing costs to line 6 on page 76.)

Insurance

What do you spend each year for the following kinds of insurance? (Most people pay their life insurance on a quarterly basis. Homeowner's insurance may be paid yearly. First, figure out the total amount you pay on an annual basis, then divide that by 12 to find out how much you spend each month.) Note: Auto insurance is provided for under the Automobile category. Health insurance is provided for under the Health Care category. House insurance is provided for under Housing Costs.

1. Life insurance, annual payment $ ____

2. Other ______________________ $ ____
   ______________________ $ ____

ANNUAL TOTAL: $ ____

Divide by 12. MONTHLY TOTAL: $ ____

(Copy monthly total to line 7 on page 76.)

*In the future I/we want to set aside $ _______ per month ($ _____ per year) in addition to the foregoing for the purpose of ______________________.

Food

The following list asks you to separate your non-food spending from your spending for real food. If you do not know how much you spend in each category, try shopping at a store that gives you an itemized cash register tape and keep all your tapes for one month to get an estimate.

REAL FOOD

Fresh produce $ ____
Dairy products $ ____
Meat, fish, eggs $ ____

Convenience foods (canned, frozen, pre-packaged)	$ ____
Bakery goods—bread, muffins, already baked	$ ____
Desserts—ice cream, cake or cake mixes, cookies, candy bars	$ ____
Snack foods—chips, dips, corn nuts, peanuts	$ ____
NON-FOODS	
Diapers	$ ____
Baby oil, powder, etc.	$ ____
Garden supplies	$ ____
Stationery, school supplies	$ ____
Magazines, newspapers	$ ____
Cleaning supplies, soap	$ ____
Household articles	$ ____
Film, batteries	$ ____
Socks, underwear, hose	$ ____
TOTAL per week	**$ ____**
Multiply by 52. ANNUAL TOTAL:	**$ ____**
Divide by 12. MONTHLY TOTAL:	**$ ____**

(Copy monthly total to line 8 on page 76.)

*In the future I/we want to set aside $ _______ per month ($ _____ per year) in addition to the foregoing for the purpose of ________________________________.

Automobile Expense

This category should include all of the costs of operating all of your vehicles. Included in the expense of your automobile is the amount you must spend to insure, maintain, repair and license it.

CAR #1 (make and model): ____________________

1. Operating Costs
   a. How many miles is car driven each year?
      ____
   b. Multiply (a) times $.30 $ ____
2. Insurance and Registration
   a. Annual registration fee $ ____
   b. Insurance—annual cost for this car $ ____
3. Car Payments
   a. Present fair market value of car $ ____
   b. Total unpaid balance on car $ ____
   c. Monthly payment x 12 $ ____

Add together (1b), (2a), (2b) and (3c).
ANNUAL TOTAL: **$ ____**

Divide by 12. MONTHLY TOTAL: **$ ____**

CAR #2 (make and model): ____________________

1. Operating Costs
   a. How many miles is car driven each year?
      ____
   b. Multiply (a) times $.30 $ ____
2. Insurance and Registration
   a. Annual registration fee $ ____
   b Insurance—annual cost for this car $ ____

3. Car Payments
   a. Present fair market value of car $ ____
   b. Total unpaid balance on car $ ____
   c. Monthly payment x 12 $ ____

Add together (1b), (2a), (2b) and (3c).
ANNUAL TOTAL: **$ ____**

Divide by 12. MONTHLY TOTAL: **$ ____**

CAR #3 (make and model): ____________________

1. Operating Costs
   a. How many miles is car driven each year?
   ____
   b. Multiply (a) times $.30 $ ____

2. Insurance and Registration
   a. Annual registration fee $ ____
   b. Insurance—annual cost for this car $ ____

3. Car Payments
   a. Present fair market value of car $ ____
   b. Total unpaid balance on car $ ____
   c. Monthly payment x 12 $ ____

Add together (1b), (2a), (2b) and (3c).
ANNUAL TOTAL: **$ ____**

Divide by 12. MONTHLY TOTAL: **$ ____**

TOTAL MONTHLY COSTS FOR ALL CARS: $ ____

(Copy monthly total to line 9 on page 76.)

*In the future I/we want to set aside $ ______ per

month ($ ____ per year) in addition to the foregoing for the purpose of ______________________________.

Clothing

1. How much do you spend on clothing for each family member annually?

Name of Each Family Member Amount Spent

____

____

____

____

____

____

Annual Total: **$ ____**

Divide by 12. Monthly Total: **$ ____**

2. How much do you spend on dry cleaning and laundry for each family member monthly?

Name of Each Family Member Amount Spent

____

____

____

____

____

____

Monthly Total: **$ ____**

Multiply by 12. Annual Total: **$ ____**

TOTAL MONTHLY COSTS OF CLOTHING: **$ ____**

(Copy monthly total to line 10 on page 76.)

*In the future I/we want to set aside $ ____ per month ($ ____ per year) in addition to the foregoing for the purpose of ______________________________.

Health Care

Write in expenses per month:

Medical care $ ____

Dental care $ ____

Prescriptions $ ____

Orthodontist $ ____

Health Insurance Premiums $ ____

MONTHLY TOTAL: **$ ____**

Multiply by 12. ANNUAL TOTAL: **$ ____**

(Copy monthly total to line 11 on page 76.)

(*)In the future I/we want to set aside $ ____ per month ($ ____ per year) in addition to the foregoing for the purpose of ______________________________.

Assistance Expenses

Amount set aside each month for:

Legal assistance $ ____

Financial assistance (e.g., bookkeeper) $ ____

MONTHLY TOTAL: **$ ____**

Multiply by 12. ANNUAL TOTAL: **$ ____**

(Copy monthly total to line 12 on page 76.)

THE SECURE LIFESTYLE COMMITMENT

Credit Card Debt Reduction

List the total balance owed, the minimum monthly payment, and the rate and amount of interest you pay on each account.

	Balance	Monthly Payment
a. Creditor name: ___________	$ ____	$ ____
Rate of interest: _____ %		
Total interest paid annually: $ ____		
b. Creditor name: ___________	$ ____	$ ____
Rate of interest: _____ %		
Total interest paid annually: $ ____		
c. Creditor name: ___________	$ ____	$ ____
Rate of interest: _____ %		
Total interest paid annually: $ ____		
d. Creditor name: ___________	$ ____	$ ____
Rate of interest: _____ %		
Total interest paid annually: $ ____		
e. Creditor name: ___________	$ ____	$ ____
Rate of interest: _____ %		
Total interest paid annually: $ ____		
f. Creditor name: ___________	$ ____	$ ____
Rate of interest: _____ %		
Total interest paid annually: $ ____		

TOTALS:
Balances **$ ____**
Monthly Payments **$ ____**

(Copy monthly total to line 13 on page 76.)

*In the future I/we want to set aside $ _______ per month ($ _____ per year) in addition to the foregoing for the purpose of ______________________________.

Secured Debt Reduction

This section includes furniture, appliances, jewelry—contracts secured by collateral. List the total balance owed, the minimum monthly payment, and the rate and amount of interest you pay on each account.

	Balance	Monthly Payment
a. Creditor name: ___________ Rate of interest: _____ % Total interest paid annually: $ ____	$ ____	$ ____
b. Creditor name: ___________ Rate of interest: _____ % Total interest paid annually: $ ____	$ ____	$ ____
c. Creditor name: ___________ Rate of interest: _____ % Total interest paid annually: $ ____	$ ____	$ ____
d. Creditor name: ___________ Rate of interest: _____ % Total interest paid annually: $ ____	$ ____	$ ____
e. Creditor name: ___________ Rate of interest: _____ % Total interest paid annually: $ ____	$ ____	$ ____

TOTALS:
Balances **$ ____**
Monthly Payments **$ ____**

(Copy monthly total to line 14 on page 76.)

*In the future I/we want to set aside $ _______ per month ($ _____ per year) in addition to the foregoing for the purpose of ____________________________.

Other Miscellaneous Debt Reduction

List below all other obligations you owe, such as medical bills, hospital bills, and loans from personal friends or relatives, etc.

Name of Creditor	Amount Owed	Monthly Pmt.
____________________	$ ____	$ ____
____________________	$ ____	$ ____
____________________	$ ____	$ ____
____________________	$ ____	$ ____
____________________	$ ____	$ ____
____________________	$ ____	$ ____
____________________	$ ____	$ ____
____________________	$ ____	$ ____
____________________	$ ____	$ ____
____________________	$ ____	$ ____

TOTALS:
Amount Owed **$ ____**
Monthly Payments **$ ____**

(Copy monthly total to line 15 on page 76.)

*In the future I/we want to set aside $ _______ per month ($ _____ per year) in addition to the foregoing for the purpose of ____________________________.

Savings

List below the amount you are currently setting aside each month in savings in each of the following categories:

Wage Security $ ____
Minimum Goal: 3 to 6 months total
(Copy monthly total to line 16 on page 76.)

Home Security $ ____
Minimum Goal: 3 months' payment or rent
(Copy monthly total to line 17 on page 76.)

Auto Security $ ____
Minimum Goal: to pay cash for next car in ____ months
(Copy monthly total to line 18 on page 76.)

Retirement/Pension $ ____
(Copy total to line 19 on page 76.)

College Fund $ ____
(Copy total to line 20 on page 76.)

Other $ ____
(Copy total to line 21 on page 76.)

*In the future I/we want to set aside $ _______ per month ($ ____ per year) in addition to the foregoing for the purpose of ______________________________.

Recapitulation of Expenses

Enter below the monthly totals from each of the categories on the previous pages.

JOYFUL LIFESTYLE includes

1. Donations and giving $ ____
2. Personal gift giving $ ____
3. Recreation, entertainment, vacations $ ____
4. Health, beauty, self-improvement $ ____
5. Animals and pets $ ____

MONTHLY SUBTOTAL:
JOYFUL LIFESTYLE COMMITMENT = $ ____

PRACTICAL LIFESTYLE includes

6.	Housing	$ ____
7.	Insurance	$ ____
8.	Food	$ ____
9.	Automobile	$ ____
10.	Clothing	$ ____
11.	Health Care	$ ____
12.	Assistance Expenses	$ ____

MONTHLY SUBTOTAL:
PRACTICAL LIFESTYLE COMMITMENT = $ ____

SECURE LIFESTYLE includes

13.	Credit card debt reduction	$ ____
14.	Secured debt reduction	$ ____
15.	Other miscellaneous debt reduction	$ ____
16.	Savings (wage security)	$ ____
17.	Savings (home security)	$ ____
18.	Savings (auto security)	$ ____
19.	Retirement/Pension	$ ____
20.	College fund	$ ____
21.	Other	$ ____

MONTHLY SUBTOTAL:
SECURE LIFESTYLE COMMITMENT = $ ____

GRAND TOTAL $ ____

TOTAL MONTHLY EXPENSES WHICH ARE NECESSARY BUT PRESENTLY NOT IN OUR BUDGET (* Items) $ ____

INCOME

Now take out your paycheck stubs or your last income tax return and write down what you have left over each year for spending purposes, after you pay all your taxes. Many people do not take taxes into account when they are figuring out how much they have available to spend each month. Others have incomes which vary from one month to the next. If your income fluctuates, it is vital that you find an average and work from that.

I have been told hundreds of times, "Oh, I don't know how much I make. It varies from one month to the next." Right there is where the trouble starts. If your take-home pay changes from one period to another, it is even more important that you take an average of your monthly pay, and that you then budget cautiously so that, during the months when the income goes down, you will not be without basic necessities.

HOUSEHOLDER #1: ____________________

Annual take-home pay $ ____

HOUSEHOLDER #2: ____________________

Annual take-home pay $ ____

Additional income from other sources: rental property, child support or alimony, freelance work, disability income (describe):

______________________________ $ ____

______________________________ $ ____

______________________________ $ ____

TOTAL ANNUAL INCOME **$ ____**

Divide by 12. TOTAL MONTHLY INCOME **$ ____**

Do your expenses exceed your income? If so, don't

panic. You already knew that, didn't you? You now have some indication of where the problem areas exist. You are getting an idea about where you need to cut back and where you need to spend more.

You are getting the information together to plan a balanced Money Makeover. The next step is to make your lifestyle expenses fit within your income with enough left over to build a secure lifestyle and make your dreams start coming true.

In the next chapter we will explore the techniques of balancing the three areas of lifestyle spending with available income . . . how to find out what kind of a spending plan is best-suited to your personality . . . how to master the nuts and bolts of a simple money system that fits your needs and your personality.

$ $ $

Suggestions for Personal and Group Study

Individuals

What have you accomplished thus far?

For a moment, review what you have already achieved. List below the specific steps you have taken, and are continuing to take, to reach your goal. Right now, don't concentrate on the work that lies ahead. Just stop to give yourself credit for what you have done so far.

Examples for those of you who find it difficult to think of anything praiseworthy about yourself:

1. You have read each page of this book up to this point, and have taken time to make notes in the margins about points you specifically want to remember and go over at a later time.

2. You are beginning to think about where you want

to be financially in a few years, and you have formed a resolve to get there.

3. You have begun assembling your own personal Budget Box according to the instructions in this chapter.

4. You have taken a tangible step toward success by filling out the Money Makeover Inventory so that you can now systematically sift, analyze and review your personal financial data. You are methodically putting together a base of data which will enable you to revise your reality to fit your vision of financial liberation.

5. You have enlisted the aid of a support group or friend to help you in this program.

Group Discussion

1. Did you find any unusual surprises when you tallied up the categories in the Money Makeover Inventory?

2. Can you see, already, some areas where you can "plug up leaks"?

3. Have one member of the group bring the latest copy of Kelley Blue Book to assist in finding automobile values. Or ask a member to write out a list of the members' vehicles; go to the library to check the Kelley Blue Book or other reference showing current fair market values of autos.

5

Your Personality and Your Money

Step 4: Discover your Money Personality.

Solvency is entirely a matter of temperament and not of income.
—Logan Pearsall Smith

Now this is what the Lord Almighty says: "Give careful thought to your ways. You have planted much, but have harvested little. You eat, but never have enough. You drink, but never have your fill. You put on clothes, but are not warm. You earn wages, only to put them in a purse with holes in it. . . .Give careful thought to your ways" (Haggai 1:5-7, NIV).

Are you trying to live up to someone else's standards on how you should be handling your money?

Oprah Winfrey says, "Most money problems come about because people are trying to be something they are not."[1] I agree.

Have you struggled to put into practice the budget systems of other self-proclaimed financial experts, only to find that they don't work for you? If all of us are so very different, why should we expect that there is one right way of managing our finances?

God teaches a lab course on human personality called Nursery 101. Most parents will tell you that they become aware of personality structure quite forcefully when they have more than one child. Two children growing up in the same home may be two very different individuals. One will be quiet and studious, the other outgoing and athletic. No amount of training or parental interference is going to change one into the other, though as parents we usually try.

The Four Personality Types

A Way to Understand Behavior— Both Yours and Others'

In recent years Florence Littauer has become an authority on personality classification, starting with her book *Personality Plus* and later, *Your Personality Tree.*[2] Florence attributes the germ of some of her ideas to Tim LaHaye; and both of these fine authors give credit to a Greek physician named Hippocrates who lived some 2,300 years ago. The personality theory of behavior has been around for a long time. Students of human behavior such as Adickes, Kretschmer, Spranger and Adler all did work in this area, but for a time the personality theory of behavior lost status. Then in the 1950s Isabel Myers and her mother Katheryn Briggs devised the Myers-Briggs Type Indicator which once more revived interest in the four temperaments.[3]

The four personality categories are based on the "core needs" which drive each of us. These needs affect all our decisions, our actions, and our life goals. In a very simple way, the four personality types might be described as follows:

The *Choleric* is primarily motivated by a desire for power.

The *Sanguine* is primarily motivated by a desire for pleasure.

The *Melancholy* is primarily motivated by a desire to achieve perfection.

The *Phlegmatic* is primarily motivated by a desire for peace.

You may have tried in the past to change to conform to the expectations or demands of others, but your basic personality is as unchanging as the color of your eyes.

What does your personality type have to do with managing your money? Everything. Your personality affects your choices and your style of dealing with conflicts. Your personality affects the way you view yourself in terms of solving problems.

An understanding of your basic personality type will help you to accept yourself and assist you in setting realistic goals. You will stop comparing yourself unfavorably with other financial "geniuses" and start maximizing your own gifts.

Furthermore, an understanding of the personality types will alter the way you perceive the other important people in your life. You will appreciate that people are the way they are, not because they were trained to be that way, took courses to be that way, or were born with moral fibre and just decided to will themselves to be the way they are. Once you understand your God-given personality type you will experience a new freedom, love and tolerance in all your personal relationships.

You will also learn how your personality type influences your money decisions. This will help you make adjustments to maximize the strengths and minimize the weaknesses that are inherent to each personality. So our next step is:

Step 4:
Discover your Money Personality.

As I describe the four personality types to you, I'm

going to paint some broad strokes. Keep in mind that real-life temperaments are rarely as black-and-white as the following descriptions may seem. But I share these ideas with you to help you understand the basic combination of positive and negative tendencies that are unique to each personality type. See if you recognize yourself among the following four characters.

Sanguine Sam

Sam has an outgoing, generous and enthusiastic Sanguine personality. He enjoys being the center of attention and can tell funny stories better than anyone else at a party. He likes groups, loves to have an audience, and hates structure. He has the ability to explain complex material in a simple and understandable way. He is not a 9-to-5 person.

Sam will do well in a career that is varied and challenging, but he will not willingly endure boredom for long. He is creative, innovative and outgoing. A born salesman, he can sell ice to Eskimos, and is just the sort of person to take part in your amateur theatrical production. He enjoys change but has trouble following rules if he considers them too rigid.

Because he hates detail, is a creature of impulse and does not like anything tedious, his checkbook is never balanced. Sam will not adhere to a regimen that requires a lot of detailed record keeping. Complicated systems that require self-discipline over long periods are simply not for him. He does have a strong sense of direction and an open mind, however, so he will change when he sees that an undesirable habit is harming his future.

Because he has a hard time setting limits or even perceiving them, he tends to be over-committed at every level. He has a willing heart to serve, but has a weak follow-through. He has a tendency to be disorganized and unreliable. He likes to volunteer for tasks, but because he has boundless enthusiasm for so many things he ends up disappointing those who depend on him.

The same is true in his financial life. He doesn't have a firm grip on the finite nature of his paycheck. He always thinks he can squeeze just one more tiny installment payment out of his salary. The result is escalating debt. Because he acts on impulse and doesn't keep records, he has no idea how much he is spending.

Is there hope for the Sanguine? Yes! The apostle Peter is sometimes described as an example of the Sanguine type of personality. In the beginning of his walk with Jesus he was undisciplined and inefficient. But Sanguines are warm-hearted and adaptable. Peter went on to become a powerful speaker, leader and church administrator, respected for his decisions and his maturity.

Choleric Carl

Carl is a powerhouse. He knows who's boss: He is! And he expects everybody else to keep that in mind at all times. It isn't that Carl is mean-spirited. He is just a born leader and doesn't want to waste a lot of valuable time explaining to people why they're wrong. He wants quick obedience and silent compliance from those around him.

Carl enjoys risk-taking, adventure and challenge. He is competitive, sharp, quick-witted and articulate. Most of all he likes to be in charge. When he becomes a part of a group, it will not be very long before he starts trying to run it. Whether this is good or bad depends on the management style he adopts. As long as he is not overly bossy, his leadership is welcomed.

Carl is highly motivated, a self-starter and confident in his decisions. All of these qualities are excellent in managers. But sometimes his competitive nature overpowers others and squelches constructive input.

Carl likes to do all the talking. He thinks he is always right, and sees no need to listen to anybody else's views on any topic. This personality trait may lead him through many difficulties before he finally learns that others also have intelligence, insight and wisdom. He will take a great leap forward in his maturity when he learns to really listen to others.

Because of his ability to envision great results and his organizational skill in taking on demanding projects, the Choleric is continually living at the limit of income in order to finance the next vision. The Choleric has the dubious ability to put at risk large sums of money very quickly in order to underwrite his latest pet ambition. Cholerics are born entrepreneurs who hate to work for others. When engaged in enterprises that excite them, they will work longer and with more intensity than any of the other personality types. But because of their unwillingness to accept input, and their sometimes nearly-manic sense of personal power, they may destroy their own dreams through unwise risk and debt.

Is there hope for the Choleric? Yes! The Choleric's uniquely creative ability to envision great things and organize to produce results, if tamed by maturity and respect for the needs of others, is the mark of great leaders in every field. The apostle Paul was probably a Choleric—domineering, organized and highly talented. Paul was used mightily by the Lord, once his talents were tempered by tolerance and humility.

Melancholy Martin

No one has a better eye for detail than Melancholy Martin. He can review pages of figures, patiently calculate the results, and happily search for mistakes. A perfectionist in almost everything he undertakes, he has the ability to find the lump in everybody else's gravy.

Martin is a stickler for detail. He tries to do The Correct Thing in every situation. A Melancholy lives by the expressions: "A right way to do everything" and "A place for everything and everything in its place."

Martin can bring order into chaos. But beneath his cool exterior he is haunted by feelings of inadequacy which bring on depression. Wanting everything to be perfect, he naturally strives for perfection in himself. By subjecting himself to his own often-unattainable standards he has the capacity for making himself and those around him quite miserable.

Martin is the kind of person by whom (and for whom) all the money management manuals and seminars are written. He should choose a career in engineering, accounting or science. Martin knows at all times where he stands financially. He rarely gets into financial trouble because by nature he is frugal and conservative, although because of his eye for perfection he may overspend in order to possess the best.

Because he is also tenderhearted and sensitive, he may unwisely co-sign loans for others, or invest in business enterprises in which he has no expertise. If he experiences a financial failure (which is uncommon because of his normally cautious nature) it may be because of excessive caution, rigidity, or resistance to change or problems with interpersonal relationships in the business scene.

Another of Martin's problems is his tendency to put off taking action until everything is perfect. This goes beyond normal prudent preparation, and becomes procrastination. In business, it can sometimes be disastrous.

Like Choleric Carl, Martin has a tendency to take his own view of things too seriously. He believes it is essential to strive for perfection and is intolerant of anyone who does not share his passion for flawlessness.

Can Melancholy Martin ever turn his life into the grand vision of perfection that taunts him? He can be better than that—he can be all God wants him to be. The New Testament writings shine with the achievements of Timothy, who was probably a Melancholy. As a young man Timothy was haunted by perfectionistic self-doubt and an introspective nature that seemed to foreshadow only moderate success.

Under the guidance of Paul and in submission to the work of the Holy Spirit in his life, Timothy became a joyous defender of the faith, a dynamic minister and brilliant writer. He was able to encourage, love and effectively guide the expansion of Christianity in new areas. Paul identified Timothy as a "kindred spirit," and commended him for his ability to serve selflessly (Philippians 2:20-23). Like all Cholerics, Paul truly began to achieve his greatest potential when he enlisted the support of a meticulous, dependable Melancholy—Timothy—to act as his good right arm.

Phlegmatic Phil

Phlegmatic Phil is one of the best people to have around. He is unflappable, good-natured, patient, self-controlled, dependable, responsible, hard-working and conscientious. He is the kind of person who smooths out the rough spots created by all the rest of us Controlling Cholerics, Perfectionistic Melancholies and Impulsive Sanguines.

Phil is not driven by a huge ego. He won't show up at your dinner party ready to see if there is dust on the top of your refrigerator or curdles in your hollandaise.

Once headed toward a goal Phil is not likely to change course. It just takes too much trouble. He hates change. He is not given to extremes of expression and in a close relationship may be accused of being unfeeling, unresponsive or uncaring.

In a management position he faithfully carries out his duties, working steadily and competently and without dazzle. He gets along well with others and is adept at easing tensions. He works under stress better than any of the other personalities. He would make an excellent counselor, teacher or physical education coach. He doesn't fall apart when a crisis occurs, nor does he demand top billing.

He is not racked by ambition, impulse, greed or judgmentalism. He may rise to the top of an organization, outdoing both the talented Choleric and the amiable Sanguine because of his ability to get along with others and not make enemies. But if faced with confrontation or challenge he may waffle or backtrack because he cannot handle anger, either his own or others'. He does not willingly take risks. He is not comfortable bucking trends, nor will he take a stand as a lone proponent of an unpopular cause.

In business matters particularly, he can sometimes be naive and short-sighted. His trusting nature may make him easy prey for unscrupulous promoters with ill-conceived deals.

Can Phlegmatic Phil reach the heights? Don't doubt him! Some people think Abraham, that mighty man of faith, was a Phlegmatic. As a seeker of peace (that primary drive of Phlegmatics) he chose Hebron rather than strife (Genesis 13:6-12). He was staunchly loyal to Lot despite the latter's serious shortcomings (Genesis 18:16-33). Because Phlegmatics find it difficult to say no and take a firm stand, at times Abraham was unduly swayed by women in his life as he sought domestic tranquility. He told his wife to pretend to be his sister out of fear of confrontation with the Egyptians (Genesis 12:11-

20). Yet Abraham was also a man of faith, dependability, courage. God chose him because he could be trusted with a mighty vision.

Personality and the Debt Trap

Your spending and saving habits are inextricably bound up with your personality. A financial plan which is designed for a detail-oriented Melancholy will not work for a free-wheeling Sanguine or a laid-back Phlegmatic. In order to understand the nature and construction of your particular debt trap, you need to understand the personality God gave you. Then and only then can you make choices which will be effective for you, because they will be suited to your unique strengths and limitations.

Years ago I lived in the San Fernando Valley in one of those homogeneous communities where everyone was young, newly married and struggling. We lived next door to Leonard and Wanda. Leonard was quiet and agreeable. He sang in the choir, worked in the yard on weekends, and was planning a lifetime career with the bank in his chosen field of accounting. He had a host of friends, was satisfied with his job, and took life pretty much as it came. He was a typical Phlegmatic.

Wanda was outspoken, talkative, and had a strong opinion on every subject. She bristled with energy, much of which was used to take over situations where Leonard was too disinterested to act. Wanda was a typical Choleric.

While Leonard was happy with things as they were, Wanda was driven to seek change and improvement, especially with regard to finances. Like most Cholerics, Wanda liked to think big. She was sure that if Leonard would only follow her instructions, they could be rich beyond her wildest dreams. In order to achieve her ambitions, she was convinced she had to fix Leonard. Leonard didn't care about getting rich; he just wanted to be left alone to prune his rose bushes.

Wanda was always trying to get Leonard to enroll in seminars and self-improvement programs. Once she persuaded him to take a two-weekend course on "How to Get Rich in Real Estate With No Money Down." The sessions were all designed and conducted by hard-driving, confident, dynamic Cholerics just like Wanda. The audiences were told how simple it was to be hard-driving, confident and dynamic. It was simple, of course, to the instructors. To them it seemed easy because they had an inborn ability to be all of those things. For Leonard it was neither natural nor effortless.

One Saturday Leonard was outside mowing his lawn while I was clipping the hedge that bordered our properties. He seemed more than normally withdrawn. We exchanged a few pleasantries and then, because we were on fairly friendly terms, I commented on his apparent gloom.

He stopped mowing and took a long, studied moment to wipe the perspiration from his forehead. "Wanda's signed us up for another one of those courses without asking me. This one is called 'How to Take Charge of Your Life,' or something." He looked straight at me. Mirth struggled to get the upper hand over anger in his face. "Why should I take charge of my life, when Wanda has it so well in hand?" His laughter did not conceal his bitterness.

It is never wise to try to be something you are not in order to keep peace with or please someone else. In the same way, when we attempt to force others into a mold which we have designed for them, we may be engaging in a cruel form of abuse.

Systems which seem simple and workable to a Melancholy might intimidate and depress a Sanguine,

Choleric or Phlegmatic. Financial freedom may be achievable in one way for Leonard, another way for Wanda, another for you or me.

Most of us find ourselves married to spouses with opposite personality characteristics. In love and in finances, opposites attract. So it is not uncommon to find that two people have completely different sets of values concerning financial issues.

If your marriage is a battleground when it comes to money, don't despair. The very contrasts which are now a basis for friction, can be a source of great strength. In chapter 11 we will discuss ways to form a partnership with your spouse.

No one personality type has a lock on financial security. There are notorious failures and world-famous successes in each of the personality types. The point is not how you are made, but what you do with the unique qualities of your own personality.

Many of us find that we are a blend of two personality types such as Choleric-Sanguine, or Melancholy-Phlegmatic, possessing some strong characteristics from each.

Which type are you?

Take the Personality Profile on the pages that follow and find out.

YOUR PERSONALITY PROFILE

Read each scenario, then circle the statement that best describes how you would respond to the situation.

1. You're thinking about balancing your checkbook.

   a. You personally enter each check, keep track of the balance, and reconcile the statement every month.

   b. You seldom know your exact bank balance.

   c. You frequently have to call up the bank to find out your bank balance.

   d. You keep a large overdraft protection and don't worry about it.

2. You think you are overdue for a raise.

   a. You redouble your efforts, get to work earlier, and work better and faster.

   b. You think it over and decide to wait and see what happens at the next salary review.

   c. You tell the boss you want a raise.

   d. You complain to your friends about being unappreciated and start thinking about getting another job.

3. Your daughter wants a $100 prom dress. You feel $60 would be more appropriate, but she persists.

   a. To avoid an argument, you give in and let her charge it.

   b. You work out a plan so she can earn the money or pay you back for a part of the purchase price.

   c. You go shopping with her and take charge of

the selection process. She ends up with a $200 dress.

d. You start feeling sentimental and nostalgic and she talks you into the $100 dress.

4. Your five-year-old car is not yet paid for, but it is beginning to have mechanical problems. You cannot afford a new car.

   a. You get a consolidation loan to lower your monthly payments and trade in the car on a model that projects a successful image.

   b. After comparison shopping you buy the best you can afford.

   c. You can't decide, so you procrastinate until it breaks down.

   d. You decide you have to have a car and you close the deal in one afternoon.

5. You have just unexpectedly inherited $50,000 from your aunt's estate. You have no children. How will you spend (or save) it?

   a. You buy clothes, furs, an auto—or something flamboyant that will amaze all your friends.

   b. You buy adult toys for yourself and lots of gifts for friends and plan a wonderful vacation cruise with your favorite friends.

   c. You deposit the money in the bank and are happy that you can loan it to friends who need it.

   d. You seek the advice of an accountant and lawyer and set up an investment portfolio, putting the rest into a living trust.

6. You have just unexpectedly inherited $50,000

from your aunt's estate. You have four children. How will you spend (or save) it?

a. You set up educational trust funds for your children so they will not be able to get the money until they are thirty years old.
b. You buy a bigger house and throw a party.
c. You hire an investment counselor and start figuring out ways to corner the soybean market so you can make it really big.
d. You have no idea, but you figure something will occur to you after you talk it over with your friends. What's the rush?

7. You have a ten-year-old daughter who shows signs of being highly gifted in mechanics.

a. You don't see any reason why she should not pursue science and also excel in other areas, so you push her to develop her musical ability too.
b. You start a college tuition savings plan but make only occasional deposits.
c. You think she's a great kid.
d. You hire a private tutor, brag about her at every opportunity, and start selecting which college she will attend.

8. You have just bought a house that is a fixer-upper, knowing that in a few years it will need a new roof.

a. You figure out what a new roof will cost in five years, divide that by sixty and start setting aside money every month to cover the cost, so that when the time comes you can pay cash and get a better deal.

b. You may not even be in this house in five years, so why worry about it now?

c. A house is an investment. You plan to make cosmetic improvements and sell the house in three years. Let the new owners worry about the roof.

d. For the same monthly outlay you decide to put in a swimming pool, which is a lot more fun than a roof.

9. Where are your important family documents such as: health and medical records, insurance policies, tax returns, deeds of trust, contracts for auto and furniture purchases, instruction booklets for appliances?

a. You're not sure exactly where they are right now, but you could probably find them.

b. You don't keep files on everything; if you ever need a copy of those things in an emergency, you would call up somebody for copies.

c. It's not your management style to deal with trivial details; you have delegated this to someone else.

d. You know where they are, and have a system for keeping them up-to-date.

10. Insurance coverage:

a. You always know where your policies are, what the coverage is, and when each policy expires.

b. You don't have any insurance or it's lapsed.

c. You know you have insurance, but you have misplaced the policies.

d. You leave all such details up to your insurance broker.

11. Income taxes:
    a. You know exactly what you paid in federal income tax last year.
    b. You didn't file your return. You usually file late or at the last minute.
    c. You filed a return, but you don't know where it is.
    d. You are in a dispute with the IRS, and the IRS is wrong.

12. Gifts:
    a. You have a budget for gift-giving and keep within it.
    b. You love to buy gifts for people. You charge most gift purchases and don't keep track.
    c. You seldom buy gifts but when you do, you don't go overboard.
    d. Because you have expensive tastes, people enjoy receiving gifts from you. You don't keep track of how much you spend annually, but it's probably too much.

13. Vacations:
    a. You haven't had a vacation in more than two years. When you do, it's to a first-class hotel, and you take work with you.
    b. Although having fun is not a high priority with you, if you do have a vacation, you plan it, save for it, and do not go over your budget.
    c. You usually don't take planned vacations; you just go places with your friends when someone else suggests it.
    d. You love vacations. You may go on short trips,

but you don't know what you spend and don't have a specific amount budgeted, but you sure have a lot of fun.

14. You have been passed over for a promotion.
    a. You don't say anything, but your withdrawn attitude lets everyone know you have been wronged. Inwardly, you feel there is something wrong with you.
    b. It's not pleasant, but isn't worth getting upset about.
    c. You have a good cry, or storm about it to your friends for an evening, then gradually get over it and go on with your life.
    d. You are mortally offended, and you immediately lay plans to find another position with a competing company.

15. Financial advisors state that you should have a written plan for your financial goals covering the next five years.
    a. When your next deal "hits big" it's going to make you rich. That, in a nutshell, is your whole plan. To strike it rich.
    b. You are having trouble picking just the right goals.
    c. You have written goals but don't follow them.
    d. You haven't really given it much thought.

16. You have just purchased a new car. When you get home and look over the contract again, you discover that you have been overcharged $100.
    a. You decide to forget it.
    b. You decide to sue (or, alternatively, you decide

that $100 is peanuts and not worth your trouble).

c. You get depressed about your own stupidity and the innate dishonesty of people.

d. You get furious and call up the salesman and yell at him. Later on you think of something really clever and cutting that you wish you had said.

17. Keeping records of tax deductions:

a. You have a system for keeping track of medical and other tax deductions, and you follow it to the letter.

b. You have a system but don't keep it up.

c. You don't have a system, but you think it's a good idea to have one.

d. You let your accountant, spouse or tax advisor worry about that.

18. You and your spouse:

a. You make all the important money decisions and like it that way.

b. It always seems that your spouse doesn't care about money management, but you seem unable to change things, even though you nag.

c. You let your spouse take care of the money—why bother yourself?

d. You get depressed about the future; there are so many things that could go wrong, and your spouse seems blissfully unaware of how important it is to plan meticulously.

19. Attitudes toward housing costs:

a. You never spend more than 35 percent of your income for housing costs.

b. You may not be able to afford to live in your present house, but it's important for the kids' sake to grow up in a nice neighborhood and the house will probably appreciate.

c. You don't care about your surroundings that much, so where you live is not crucially important to you personally.

d. It's important to live in a fine neighborhood if you want to move in the right social circles and be a success. You will spend whatever that takes.

20. Savings:

a. You save a specific amount from every pay period.

b. You opened a savings account some time ago and made a few deposits but it's inactive right now.

c. You haven't thought about it seriously.

d. You don't save right now. All your money is earmarked for a big deal or big purchase.

21. Clothing. Which reflects your basic attitude?

a. Looks and fashion first, quality second, cost third.

b. I don't know what I want until I see it and if I don't have the money, I charge.

c. A very few highest-quality clothes are a good investment.

d. Clothes aren't that big a deal.

22. Of the following tasks, which would you prefer if the salaries were all equal?

    a. Accountant or lab analyst or editor
    b. Sales manager or actor or rock singer
    c. Photographer or mechanic or school counselor
    d. Senator or inventor or corporation president

23. How would you describe the work area you presently control?

    a. A place for everything and everything in its place.
    b. Cluttered and disorganized, but comfortable
    c. Photographs, plants, momentoes reflecting ME
    d. Functional, impersonal, effective

24. Which of the following is most true of you at work?

    a. You have trouble getting to work on time.
    b. You arrive early, stay late, the office workhorse.
    c. You spend time chatting, socializing.
    d. Your work is your life.

How to Find Your Score

Circle the answers you selected from each question, then add the totals for each column.

	Choleric	Sanguine	Melancholy	Phlegmatic
1.	d	c	a	b
2.	c	d	a	b
3.	c	d	b	a
4.	a	d	b	c
5.	a	b	d	c
6.	c	b	a	d
7.	d	b	a	c
8.	c	d	a	b
9.	c	a	d	b
10.	d	c	a	b
11.	d	c	a	b
12.	d	b	a	c
13.	a	d	b	c
14.	d	c	a	b
15.	a	c	b	d
16.	b	d	c	a
17.	d	b	a	c
18.	a	b	d	c
19.	d	b	a	c
20.	d	b	a	c
21.	a	b	c	d
22.	d	b	a	c
23.	d	c	a	b
24.	d	c	b	a
	_____	_____	_____	_____

Total up your score in each column. The column with the highest score indicates your predominant personality type or types. You may find you are a blend of two!

$ $ $

Suggestions for Personal and Group Study

Individuals

Take the Personality Profile. What type of personality are you? Did your test results indicate you have two predominant types, such as Choleric-Sanguine or Melancholy-Phlegmatic?

Groups

1. As a group, compare the results of your personality questionnaires.
2. Have each member of the group in turn reveal his/her personality type, and what financial strengths or limitations were brought to light.
3. After each member tells the result of his personal self-study, ask the other members to affirm good personality characteristics that they have noticed about the group member who has just shared. Remember, this is a time for positive input, not criticism. As each individual tells about himself/herself, allow plenty of time for the rest of the group to point out specific strengths and good qualities that relate to that person's virtues. For instance, a Choleric personality might reveal his problems with wanting to unreasonably manipulate others. The members of the group, however, might have noticed that he is also creative, supportive, fun to be around, etc.

6

The Money Makeover Network

Step 5: Network with people of opposite temperament.

We are meant to be addicted to God,
but we develop secondary addictions
that temporarily appear to fix our problems.
—Edward M. Berckman

Owe no man anything (Romans 13:8, NKJV).

Have you ever noticed how secretive most of us are about money troubles?

Most of us would rather get hit by a truck than discuss our financial problems. Yet this is one area where working with others—particularly those who will not automatically and reverentially agree with us—is vitally important.

I am going to suggest something that may seem unnatural to you at first. I am going to propose that you work cooperatively with at least one other person in making financial decisions. If you are married, I recommend that you find a third person (and a fourth, if possible), to act as a financial advisor.

The reason for this is very simple.

When you took your Personality Profile, and perhaps even before you picked up this book, you realized you had certain shortcomings when it comes to making financial moves. Some of these are a matter of poor habits or low motivation or lack of information. You can change those. Other behaviors are related to the way you are as a person. Those things are never going to change. If you have hated numbers all your life, I am not going to be able to change you into a CPA by the time you finish reading this chapter.

So what can you do?

Step 5:
Network with people of opposite temperament.

No matter what your personality type, this step applies to you. It may be the simplest and most important aspect of your recovery program. Find the specific steps below which relate to your particular personality type. Experiment with my suggestions. As you develop a money management system in keeping with your personality, you will undoubtedly come up with new and innovative ideas. If you would like to share those ideas with me, I would be delighted to hear from you. You can write to me at P. O. Box 4085, Crestline, CA 92325.

Jack's Story: The Sanguine Debts to Find Pleasure

Jack and Laurie seemed like the ideal couple. They were young, athletic and outgoing. Jack, especially, seemed to have a witty response to every question I asked him during our first interview. Though they were deeply in debt, he appeared to be emotionally detached from their problems.

Their Money Makeover Inventory revealed they were spending a disproportionately high amount of their income in the area of a Joyful Lifestyle. Jack was a Sanguine with a seemingly insatiable appetite for fun.

Laurie grumbled a little, good-naturedly, but I could see there was resentment lurking behind her light-hearted words. "You should just *see* our garage and back yard. Jack has jet skis, fishing gear, scuba equipment. And a boat."

"I guess you could say I'm a water freak," Jack said, smiling.

"You say that as though it were amusing," I interjected, "but this preoccupation with play has caused you considerable trouble with your creditors. And it's not helping your marriage either, is it? Your wife seems angry with you, although she's trying hard to be polite about what is happening."

"I like to have fun on the weekends," he admitted reluctantly. "When I want something I buy it."

Laurie was more philosophical. "We got married right out of high school. I think we got into trouble because we had never been on our own before. At first it was kind of exciting not having any parents around to tell us what to do with our money. We went overboard using credit. Pretty soon I could see we were getting into trouble, and I wanted to stop. But Jack kept telling me not to worry, and he kept right on charging. Now we're late on everything, we have an eviction notice, and we're getting calls from creditors."

"Jack, did Laurie ever challenge you about this before things got desperate?" I asked.

"Once in a while she would drop a little comment, but she never really put her foot down."

"I didn't really tell him the way I felt. I wanted him to be happy," Laurie admitted. "My parents always fought about bills before they got divorced. I didn't want to be a nag the way my mother was."

As we talked further, Laurie revealed that she had been raised to think the wife should leave money management entirely to her husband. To Laurie that included letting him have the entire say on how the money was spent, even when his decisions hurt their future. She and Jack had not yet formed a financial partnership. They were not even sure how this could be done.

The Sanguine Solution

Jack and Laurie agreed to take the following steps to improve their financial condition.

1. Form a Team With a Melancholy

The first and most important step in changing their financial future was for this couple to start working together as a team. The secret to putting structure in the fun-loving, impulsive Sanguine's life is to delegate responsibility to another who excels in detail and organization. In other words, a Melancholy.

Jack was fortunate to be married to Laurie, who had a Melancholy's good brain but was afraid to use it. When they began scheduling regular weekly discussions on their finances, Laurie began to see that her talents could be used to help her husband in essential ways. From the beginning of their marriage, Laurie had tried to take care of the record keeping and bill paying. Now, in addition, Laurie agreed to be more candid and vocal about financial concerns so that Jack would have her input on money matters. Laurie began to appreciate that God had given her a gift for prudent planning, which He wanted her to use actively to help her husband, who had other gifts to bring to their marriage. Jack agreed to listen to Laurie's input and promised not to make purchases unless both were in full agreement.

It isn't necessary to have a Melancholy spouse to

bring order into your life. If you are single, or if your Melancholy spouse does not want to take over the chores of bill paying and record keeping, there are bookkeeping services which will pay your bills and balance your checkbook for a reasonable monthly fee. You may have a friend or a relative who will take over this task for you. Perhaps you can hire an accountant, secretary or business manager to protect you from your impetuous nature.

2. Sidetrack Impulse Buying

Credit buying is harmful, addictive and the first no-no on the Money Makeover that applies to all personality types. But for Sanguines, who are creatures of impulse, it may be especially hard to quit debting, cold turkey. To put credit cards into the hands of a Sanguine can be almost as dangerous as letting an alcoholic carry a bottle of whiskey in his pocket. Credit buying can be powerfully addictive.

Jack knew that he should not carry excess cash or credit cards. First he and Laurie cut up their credit cards. Jack let Laurie pay the bills, and he stopped carrying a checkbook. To curb his tendency to buy on sight, he decided to carry only a $20 bill in his wallet for emergencies.

3. Include Joy in the Budget Plan

Sanguines need pleasure and people, so long-term austerity programs won't work. A Sanguine may start out with the best intentions to put every penny into savings or debt retirement, but eventually he will falter under the weight of so much inflexibility. To succeed, a budget plan for Sanguines must include a liberal sprinkling of festivity. If too strictly deprived of spending in the Joyful Lifestyle area, a Sanguine will lose heart and abandon the spending plan entirely.

Laurie previously had not participated in the activities that Jack relished, so she had to struggle to overcome her normal tendency to be reclusive and shy. She knew that Jack was working to change in order to make their relationship work, and she determined to change too. Laurie and Jack agreed that, while they would put a curb on major expenditures for adult "toys," they would make certain that having fun was a planned part of their lives. "Fun" did not necessarily mean "spending."

After she saw that her husband's personality craved merriment, just as her personality craved order, Laurie agreed to bend a little. She found low-cost ways to entertain friends by putting on dessert suppers and backyard dinners. She and Jack began to explore leisure activities that were inexpensive or free. Laurie made every effort to participate fully, knowing that by her presence she was helping Jack maintain a healthy balance and control.

They sold their boat (for less than Jack thought it was worth), but arranged to continue their periodic trips to the river with other couples by sharing the cost and renting a boat. With the money realized from the sale of the boat they were able to pay off some of their more pressing credit card obligations.

4. Make Saving Automatic

Sanguines should take full advantage of every available mechanism to make saving effortless and routine. Since Sanguines are great on making resolutions but are weak on follow-through, automatic payroll deductions make it easier to stick with the program.

After deciding on an amount they wanted to set aside from each paycheck, Jack signed up for an automatic payroll deduction through his credit union. In addition, Laurie opened a second savings account for emergencies, using an automatic checking account deduction at their bank.

Jack had previously complained privately that his wife was crabby and unresponsive. When he began to appreciate Laurie's Melancholy need for stability, this too began to change. Melancholies need to know their bills are paid on time and that there is enough set aside for emergencies. They cannot live happily without this assurance. When Laurie's needs for security and order were met, she was no longer sour, anxious and depressed. She was able to respond joyfully to Jack in the ways that he needed.

Jack and Laurie proved that "two personality types are better than one." By combining their strengths and recognizing their limitations, they grew and became the powerful team God had intended them to be when He put them together.

Betty's Story: The Choleric Debts to Gain Power

"I don't want to file bankruptcy. I just need some financial counseling."

Those were the first words Betty spoke when she sat down in my office for our first interview. She was fashionably dressed, coiffed and manicured. She looked like a woman on her way to the top, who knew exactly where she was going and how to get there. Not so, however.

Against the advice of her accountant, Betty has used a $15,000 inheritance and a $35,000 personal line of credit to embark on a lifelong dream: to own and operate her own restaurant. Betty found the perfect space in an industrial park and launched The Sandwich Enterprise. Her specialty was thick, juicy sandwiches using choice ingredients, and hearty soups made from farm-fresh vegetables. She thought she had a sure-fire money maker, and rejected all thoughts of failure. Like many Cholerics, she underestimated the risk and did not seek (and follow) advice.

At first The Sandwich Enterprise boomed as office workers and executives from neighboring businesses lined up to sample the new food sensation. But within a few months the novelty wore off, and business slowed. Betty discovered one of her employees had been stealing meat from the freezer, and fired her. The business was barely breaking even. Betty went to her bank and extended her credit line still further, pledging the equity in her home as collateral to start an advertising campaign. As a hedge, just in case business did not improve, she listed the restaurant for sale with a business opportunity broker. Betty quickly discovered that a business that is losing money is not easy to sell.

Solutions were not readily available. Even if Betty closed the business, there would be debts left over that would take years to pay. Her creditors were not interested in waiting that long. Unable to make payments on the bank loan, she was now facing the loss of her home, which had been pledged as collateral.

The Choleric Solution

Betty had urgent problems which could only be solved by legal intervention. In order to save her home from sale by creditors and allow her time to pay off her debts, a petition under Chapter 11 of the Bankruptcy Code was filed and a plan of reorganization which paid off all of her creditors over six years was approved by the court. The most important changes were brought about by Betty personally as she worked to bring about attitude and behavior changes in her life.

1. Team Up With a Melancholy

Just like Sanguine Jack, Betty needed a solid

Melancholy in her life to get her back on track. Even though previously she had not followed his advice, her Melancholy accountant was glad to take her back as a paying client. In addition, Betty found among her church acquaintances a trustworthy woman who seemed to possess all the granite characteristics of the Melancholy personality. Betty nurtured this relationship and eventually the two became good friends.

Betty frankly admitted to her new friend that she had qualities she wanted to emulate. Far from being offended or feeling used, Betty's friend was flattered and readily agreed to be Betty's touchstone. She has joined a covenant group at her church which meets weekly to provide mutual support and prayer. In this group Betty is a valued participant because of her business experience, her courage and her free flow of creative ideas. She also has added immeasurably to her resources by having input from many origins to balance, bolster and strengthen her.

2. Work on Spiritual Growth

In chapter 12 we will explore some of the reasons why all four personality types, no matter what their money problems, should give extra attention to their spiritual growth in any program to bring about change. For the Choleric, this admonition has even greater urgency. Why? Because Cholerics are people of action. They are goal-oriented, dynamic go-getters. Because they are so involved in the task at hand, they can easily fall into the habit of neglecting the sacred aspects of life. While the ego thrives, the soul withers. For the Choleric, special attention should be given to daily devotions and all of the disciplines of the faith.

The biggest challenge for Betty was to learn to accept input from others, which she did by joining the covenant/study group at her church. Accepting input from sources outside herself included expanding her spiritual base.

In her covenant group Betty discovered that she, like many Cholerics and Sanguines, needed to guard against settling for just the public demonstrations of faith. In the past she had been so action-oriented she tended to slip into the pattern of thinking she had "taken care of God" by putting in time at church services. She had neglected the reflective, solitary aspects of communicating with God in private. In prayer time, Cholerics need to spend time *listening* to God, and not just talking to Him. This takes time, patience, and what the Quakers call "centering down"—tuning out all the mental chatter so that God's voice can be heard. To do this, Betty began to devote the first twenty minutes of every day to prayer, reading and reflecting.

3. Find Joy in Helping Others

As the spiritual side of her personality grew, Betty became more aware that her life previously had been centered on herself. Being a person of action, she immediately undertook to change. She began volunteering a few hours a week at a nearby shelter for battered women.

Betty was astonished to find that her spiritual disciplines had a direct impact on her money. She visited me a few weeks later with interesting news.

"I've found some people who are helping me put together a grant proposal to open a store-front school. We'll help battered women rebuild their lives by getting practical skills—how to fill out job applications, dress for work, and go on interviews. We'll teach basic typing and office skills, and help them find jobs." As she was leaving, she hugged me and exclaimed, "I've never been so happy."

Betty agreed to make a commitment to include in her life more time for joy, less work, and more sensitivity and openness to the needs of others. Her spiritual exercises helped her recognize her tendency to egocentricity and lack of compassion, which were throwing her personality (and her finances) out of balance.

Cholerics can always turn tragedy into triumph. When Betty became sensitive to the suffering world outside her doors, she became the potent force for change that she was intended to be.

Darren's Story: The Melancholy Debts to Attain Perfection

People with Melancholy personalities seldom have money problems. That is probably because they are not impetuous, adventurous or lazy. They usually know where every penny goes, and have thought about its destination.

However, no one personality type is immune to folly. Melancholies occasionally fall into the credit trap. Darren was one such loser in the debting game. It wasn't that his salary as a management trainee was so low. It was just that Darren was the only son of a well-to-do family, accustomed to having the best of everything. Darren was not prepared for the shock of the high cost of earning his own living.

When he left home and moved into his own apartment, he found he was not able to afford all of the things he had taken for granted when he was living under his parent's roof. He began to receive credit cards in the mail, but at first didn't want to use them. (His father had always cautioned about the dangers of credit.) He promised himself he would use the cards only in an emergency.

Darren wanted very much to do the right thing. But there were so many things he needed to buy: furniture, appliances, groceries, light bulbs and vitamins. Things he had never given much thought to before. The credit cards were a convenient solution, just a stopgap until his prospects at work improved.

Within a short time he had charged several thousand dollars in merchandise, and was finding it difficult to make even the minimum monthly payment on the accounts.

Things were not going well at work, either. He was responsible for the supervision of four clerk-typists and the administration of the company's health insurance program. Darren had the ability to spot mistakes in his subordinates' work, but he had not developed a tactful way of helping them improve. He was convinced there was one right way of doing everything. Even though he was eager to share his insights with others, because of his abrupt and superior attitude, they were not receptive to his criticism. One employee quit because she said she couldn't work with him.

The head of the department soon saw that Darren's personality traits turned off, rather than motivated, the other department personnel. This cost Darren a job promotion that he had expected as well as a much-needed raise.

Darren's personality traits, unimpeded, were a liability to his company as well as to himself. Like the rest of us, his worst enemy was within.

The Melancholy Solution

Darren changed his financial future with the following mix of decisions:

1. Team Up With a Choleric and/or a Sanguine

The Melancholy needs at least two advisors who will put a brake on his obsessive need for perfection, draw him out of himself, and help him see the brighter side of things. Darren preferred to take care of all his own record keeping. He was so meticulous and detail-oriented he felt no one could do it as well as he (and he was right about this).

After analyzing his personality traits, he recognized that his job performance was hampered by attitudes of hyper-perfectionism and a tendency to be aloof. He began to consciously nurture relationships and reach out with appreciation instead of criticism. He started to hold back from making sarcastic, cutting remarks that he found amusing but which wounded or offended others.

In his characteristically focused and organized manner, Darren started seeking the company of friends who had Sanguine, Phlegmatic and Choleric temperaments.

2. Release Yourself and Others From Perfectionism

Darren worked on releasing himself and others from the vise of his hyper-perfectionism. As he learned tolerance for the mistakes of others he began to be more accepting of his own shortcomings. As he accepted imperfection as a natural fact of life, he found he no longer needed to own the best of everything. He was able to live within his means and give up credit buying. It was not hard for Darren to do this because, true to his cautious nature, he had never felt comfortable with the concept of buying things on credit.

3. Take Action Against Depression and Procrastination

Like many Melancholics, Darren had a low opinion of himself coupled with a need to achieve perfection. Because everything had to be just right, he often postponed taking necessary action out of fear that the time was not right or the outcome would not be perfect. The result was chronic despair, much like the low-grade fever one experiences from an infection—so slight it is hardly noticeable, but no less dangerous. He was able to see the links between dejection, perfectionism and overspending (buying on credit).

As Darren began to be less uptight in personal relationships, he saw more value in social skills. He sought ways to improve himself as a companion to others. This meant giving up the rigid, authoritarian and judgmental exterior he presented to the world. It also meant developing ways to interact with others in relaxed play situations. He learned to dance and water-ski. He found he didn't really enjoy these activities, but went on to become proficient at chess and tennis.

He found that physical activity had a beneficial effect on his ongoing tendency toward negativity. As a result, he became an avid runner and joined a local running club. He is now running 10K races and wins prizes in his age group. The physical, mental, emotional and social benefits are enormous—he seems to be a different person.

Like the Choleric, the Melancholy personality can become so thing- and action-oriented that this person loses sight of the Joyful Lifestyle Commitment that is essential for financial balance. Melancholies usually have no problem arranging for the Practical and Secure aspects of this lifestyle triad. They need to make a conscious effort to use money to bring spontaneity and fun to their own lives and the lives of those they love.

Darren's spending plan was woefully lacking in joy. After he paid off his credit cards he opened a savings account and made plans for the following summer to go on a two-week foreign mission with other young singles. On that trip he met a young woman of similar spiritual beliefs who has become very important to him.

4. Use Talents as Tools for Loving Others

People with Melancholy temperaments tend to hide

their feelings and isolate themselves. Darren realized this shortcoming and worked to become, instead, a bridge builder of communication and caring. He was talented in his ability to organize and enjoyed working with spreadsheets, charts and graphs, but he was impatient with those not similarly gifted. When he saw that his intolerance was costing him money through lost job opportunities and raises, he was motivated to change.

Instead of using his talents as a defense to hide his social insecurity, he began to view them as God-given gifts to be used in service to others. This shift in orientation from Super Corrector to Servant Helper made an enormous change in his relationships at work and at play. Soon others began to respond to him in a positive way. When the Melancholy incorporates warmth into his personality, he is the most valued of employees, the most trusted of advisors.

When Darren changed his attitudes and learned to accept himself and others, his finances changed. He received a job promotion, he got out of debt, and he formed the lasting, loving relationship that he had quietly yearned for all his life.

Marella's Story: The Phlegmatic Debts to Keep Peace

The Phlegmatic personality is a friend indeed. Phlegmatics would do anything for those they love. Even against their better judgment, they frequently help those who should not be asking for assistance.

"You're so good to us, we don't know what we would do without you." These words were music to Marella's ears. Unfortunately, she usually heard them after she had just made an interest-free loan to one of her friends, or co-signed a note for a relative.

When Marella came to see me she was afraid to

answer the telephone because of the creditors who were harassing her. She had run up thousands of dollars in debts, mostly for gifts. After agreeing to co-sign an automobile loan for her nephew, he fell behind on payments and the car was repossessed. Now the lender was suing Marella.

Hard-working, responsible Marella was a wonderful Phlegmatic personality with one serious fault. She couldn't say no. Marella was stingy about spending money on herself, but perfectly willing to splurge for others.

Now, at age fifty-five, she was beginning to see the pattern that had developed in her life.

"I've made myself the doormat in just about every relationship I've ever had. It's hard for me to stand up for my rights. I'm always afraid I'll get mad, so I just keep my feelings to myself."

Devoted to friends and family, she had sacrificed her own financial well-being in order to help loved ones. As a result, her own credit was ruined. She thought she could find fulfillment in living to please others. She busied herself spoiling others, doing things for them they ought to do for themselves, while putting off the decisions that would improve her own life.

Phlegmatics love to feel needed. More than any other personality type, they are pushovers for what I call the "warm fuzzies." They will do anything, give up anything, as long as they get stroked in exchange. Like starving kittens, they will purr as long as they are petted.

While the Choleric is out conquering the world, the Melancholy is correcting it and the Sanguine is cavorting in it, the Phlegmatic is cuddling it.

There is nothing wrong with warm fuzzies, as long as the necessary business of life is also receiving some attention. Marella, like all Phlegmatics, had difficulty thinking in future terms. As long as today was pleasant, everything was as it should be. Furthermore, because of her dislike of change, it was always easier to go along with whatever program anybody proposed. She was easy to get along with . . . too easy. The result was that she did not attend to the hard decisions of her own life, content to let others control her destiny.

Marella was the best friend to others, but her lackadaisical attitudes cost her dearly in lost opportunities. She had always believed that her soft, laid-back response to life's challenges was how a nice person should behave.

One morning in her church, her pastor preached on the topic of responsibility. He pointed out that we are responsible to God for our wasted time, lost opportunities, and bungled prospects. He closed his sermon with a discourse on the parable of the (wasted) talents. For the first time, Marella saw that this Bible story is especially meaningful for Phlegmatics. She began to appreciate that God was not happy with her passive waste of time, money and opportunities.

The Phlegmatic Solution

Marella brought about a dynamic change in her life and her finances when she began to network and counter-balance some of her negative traits.

1. Learn to Say No

Marella learned to master the skill of shaking her head from side to side and uttering that most difficult of all one-syllable words, "no." It's not easy to change the habits of a lifetime. She did so by reminding herself of the parable of the wasted talents, and trusting God to give her strength to change.

Through a discussion group she learned ways to express her opinions honestly and without fear. She discovered that, like many Phlegmatics, she was a "natural" to pick up co-dependency habits in relationships. She began to examine her past behaviors and question why she had settled for "victim and rescuer" roles in friendships instead of healthy give-and-take.

She has learned to let the chronic borrowers find their own way and learn their own lessons, hard though these lessons might be. Marella is in charge of her life now, and no longer sees herself as a doormat.

Learning to say no to others, she found, was the impetus she needed to begin to say yes to herself. This affected her finances in a profound way. She began to look at the continuum of her life as having not only a past and present, but also a future.

2. Network With a Choleric

When Marella began to study the personalities, she found that some of the people she admired most were Melancholies. She loved their orderly demeanor. At the same time, she noticed that Melancholy personalities tended to further depress and inactivate her. Their very perfectionism defeated her to the point that, just by observing them, she was pushed further into immobility. She needed the emotional boost that an up-beat Choleric could give her.

She "tried on" some of their attitudes, just to see how they felt. She opened her mind to accept a more dynamic, winning, active mindset. As a result, she found she had something she could learn from this other point of view. She watched the way Choleric friends put feet on their dreams, the way they got things done. She began putting some of these habits into practice in her own life.

But she also continued to need the input she could only get from the fastidious nature of a Melancholy. By surrounding herself with action-oriented Cholerics and meticulous Melancholies, Marella began to be influenced in a positive way to take effective action for change.

Marella will never become a Choleric or a Melancholy—we're glad of that. But she can watch, learn and grow from them, and improve her own life in the process.

3. Automate Savings

Like the Sanguine, Marella had problems in motivating herself to get started on a savings program. She signed up for an automatic payroll deduction plan through her company credit union and was able to stick with her program faithfully. Unlike the Sanguine who jumps from one thing to the next, the Phlegmatic does not like change and will pursue a program once it is instituted.

4. Fight Procrastination

Marella admitted that one of her greatest problems was her tendency to put off doing what needed to be done, but she knew she could be best motivated by a group of people whom she liked. Marella enlisted the help of a few of her many friends, and together they began to get together regularly for brunch to discuss their financial goals. They are pledged to help each other keep on forming realistic goals, and following through.

Follow-through is one of the most difficult areas for Marella. Since she knows that she is profoundly influenced by the company she keeps, she makes it a point to choose her friendships carefully. She reinforces her tendency toward inaction by being receptive to the input of people with Choleric tendencies who inspire her to perform, take action, and assume control over her life.

5. Emphasize the Secure Lifestyle Commitment

Because Marella was always thinking of others, she rarely thought in practical terms about her future. The whole area of The Secure Lifestyle Commitment was deficient in her spending plan (or non-plan, as she called it). Just as for Sanguine Jack, an automatic payroll savings deduction and low-risk, passive types of investments which do not require a great deal of personal involvement are good ways for a Phlegmatic personality to establish an investment program. Marella did just that.

Later on, as Marella developed more confidence, she became enthusiastic about acquiring a diversified investment portfolio. In the meantime, she continues her savings program and no longer co-signs for others or takes on new debt for herself.

With Marella's new beliefs and attitudes, she seems younger and more vibrant. She is more fun to be around. She has new interests in life and people are drawn to her calmness, stability and wisdom.

She has more friends than anyone I know—friends who respect her for her achievements and love her for her unique gifts . . . not for what she will do for them. Part of the reason for the change in her life is the new way she deals with her money. Getting control of her money really was the first step in getting control of her life.

Are You a Compulsive Overspender?

People who have chronic debt problems are sometimes angry, hurt people who try to use their checkbooks to ease the pain in their lives. If you have no control over your spending, or if you have had debt problems for many years, your difficulties may not be related to personality traits.

If your spending takes any of the following forms, you should seek help from a trained counselor with whom you can discuss not only your money but also the reasons why your spending is out of control.

- You spend to deal with depression.
- You spend to impress others.
- You spend out of spite for a wrong committed by a loved one.
- You spend to manipulate others (through gifts, etc.).
- You spend to escape reality.
- You spend to win love or acceptance.
- You spend because you cannot say no to requests or demands of others.
- You spend to make others envious.

The emotionally hurting person uses money to manipulate relationships, present a facade of importance to the outside world, and even fool herself. Money is a weapon that can be used to make others jealous or to get revenge for past hurts. Money enables us to control or dominate others (effectively hiding our anger) by bestowing presents or loans.

All of us experience occasional feelings of low self-worth, jealousy, pain, discontent, anger or guilt. And all of us have at some point gone overboard in our spending and later regretted it. But if you are heavily in debt and cannot seem to stop spending, you need spiritual and psychological counseling to get to the roots of your out-of-control behavior.

If you cannot find a competent advisor, there are self-help organizations available in many communities. One, Debtors Anonymous, operates on the principles of the Twelve-Step program of Alcoholics Anonymous. If you cannot find such a group, consider starting one at your work, neighborhood or church. In chapter 8 I will give you further information about these self-help groups.

Your checkbook reveals what is important to you. If your finances are in trouble, it is a sure sign that other areas of your life are in disarray too. It's not too late to restructure your finances and your life.

How can you get out of debt?

How can you rebuild a shattered credit rating and start over?

How much debt is too much debt?

We'll cover the answers to these questions, and more, in the next chapter as we build a spending plan that fits your unique needs.

$ $ $

Suggestions for Personal and Group Study

Individuals

1. Make a list of the ways your personality is a financial asset to you. (e.g., self-confidence, ambition, organization, etc.)

2. Make a list of the ways your personality has hindered you financially. (e.g., procrastination, sloppy record-keeping, lack of self-discipline, etc.)

3. Make a list of specific steps you can take this week to bring greater order to your finances. Set a

deadline for achieving these goals. Share your goals with a friend and ask the friend to check up on your progress to see if you have achieved your objectives by your deadline.

Group Discussion

1. Have each member of the group select a specific area of personality growth that they wish to work on, and tell about the precise steps they plan to take to improve. In the following weeks, spend five minutes having each member report to the group how they have fared in their efforts to change. (Or have the group divide up into smaller groups and report on progress.)

7

The Balancing Act

Step 6: Keep consumer debt below 20 percent of spendable income.

You've removed most of the road blocks to success when you have learned the difference between motion and direction.
—Bill Copeland

But be doers of the word, and not hearers only, deceiving yourselves. (James 1:22, RSV).

My secretary buzzed me on the intercom and announced, "Your two o'clock appointment is here."

That's not particularly unusual at two in the afternoon, but there was a tinge of amusement in her voice that made me suspicious. I asked her to show the client into my office.

"Oh-*kaaay!*"

A moment later she ushered in a weary-looking man carrying a large brown shopping bag. After exchanging the customary greetings, he explained to me what I had suspected all along—he had come to see me concerning his bills.

"Do you have a list?" I asked.

"Better than that. I brought them with me." With that he upended the bag and bills—hundreds of them—tumbled out onto the desk and spilled to the floor.

He was demonstrating a system of bookkeeping

called the Shopping Bag Method. It's a particular favorite of some of us who have trouble keeping track of our bills. It's just a step away from the Kitchen Junk Drawer Method.

I got out my calculator and began adding up the bills. The final tally was $28,139. His monthly take-home pay (spendable income after taxes and other deductions) was $1,790 or roughly $21,480 per year.

To find out the percentage of spendable income his bills represented, I divided his take-home pay by his installment debts.

$$\$28{,}139\text{ (debts)} \div \$21{,}480 = 1.31 = 131\%$$

His installment debts were equal to 131 percent of his spendable income.

Many financial counselors and loan officers advise that consumer debt (all debt—including auto loans—other than a home mortgage) should be limited to no more than 20 percent of spendable income. With a net (after-tax) income of $21,480, his allowable debt limit was just $4,296 for all debts.

When I told him he had $23,843 more in debts than he could afford, he was amazed. No one had ever told him about the 20 percent rule, which is:

Step 6:
Keep consumer debt below 20 percent of spendable income.

Do you know how much consumer debt is too much for you? Take a moment and figure it out.

What Is Your Consumer Debt Limit?

List below your monthly take-home pay.

Husband's earnings	$ ____
Wife's earnings	$ ____
Other income	$ ____
Total monthly spendable income:	$ ____

x 12 = $ ____ annual spendable income

x .20 = $ ____ consumer debt limit

Most people with debt problems gasp in disbelief when they hear this principle for the first time. They have been so accustomed to using credit that they have no idea how much debt is too much.

Many financial counselors recommend that you carry no debt at all, except for a home mortgage. I personally agree with that philosophy, but find that for many people such a goal at first seems totally unattainable. For that reason, I advise that you make 20 percent your upper debt limit to start with, and then work toward the ideal of being absolutely debt-free.

We live in a credit-mad society. The person selling you a car on credit is anxious to close the deal to earn his commission. The credit card company is anxious to garner your purchases and earn the 20 percent (or more) in annual interest you will pay on the obligation.

Buying on credit, even a little at a time, can cost you more than you imagine.

If you charge $125 each month, you will owe $7,500 at the end of five years. If you then pay off that obligation at $125 per month, it can take fifteen years to pay off the debt with interest.

A little bit of overspending adds up to years of

bondage. Imagine a newly married couple with a three-year-old child. They spend $125 more than they earn every month, charging that amount for just five years. They start to pay off the debt at the rate it was accumulated—that is, $125 per month. At that rate they will not pay off the debt until their child is ready for college. Such is the nature of credit card interest!

How Much Should You Debt for Your Home?

It is the dream of most people to own their own home. It is an emotional investment as well as a financial one. Many of us are willing to cut back in other areas just for the thrill of knowing that we have a little place on this earth that is our very own.

As a general rule, you should not have a mortgage that is more than 2.5 times your gross annual salary, or twice your net annual salary. If your gross income is $50,000 annually, that means your home mortgage should not exceed $125,000. Some financial counselors advise that your home mortgage should not exceed 1.5 times your annual gross salary, while others say you can go as high as three times your gross salary. From my experience, however, I will stick to my figure of 2.5 as a prudent guideline for most people.

Your home loan should be considered separately from other installment debt. A home is generally considered to be an appreciating asset—that is, it is expected to increase in value over a period of years. Your automobile and television set, on the other hand, are depreciating assets. They are worth less every year.

How To Balance Your Expenses and Your Income

By focusing on the three tiers of the Money Makeover (Joyful, Practical and Secure Lifestyle Commitments), you can tell at a glance if your spending is out of control or overbalanced in one area or another.

There is another way to tell if your spending is out of balance. If you are fighting about money, if creditors are calling you, if you feel unfulfilled or anxious, your spending is unbalanced in one or more of the areas.

Many people worry about what percentage of their income should be spent on various categories such as clothing, food, automobile, and so on. Perhaps you are overspending in the area of Joyful Lifestyle. Rather than tell you that you should spend a fixed percentage of 5 percent for entertainment, I would much rather advise you to try to achieve balance over the three areas of your spending with one exception. Because housing consumes such a large portion of most people's income, I advise that total housing expenditures should never exceed 35 percent of spendable income.

What Is Your Allowable Housing Cost?

In the space below, figure your allowable housing costs by taking your annual spendable income from page 77 and multiplying by .35. The result is the maximum you should be spending annually on your housing, including utilities, furnishings, fire or homeowner's insurance, and all of the items listed under Housing Costs in the Money Makeover Inventory.

Annual spendable income: $____

x .35 = $____ total allowable housing costs

In the Money Makeover Inventory you listed all expenses related to the cost of operating your residence. You included utilities, insurance, upkeep, furniture, as well as rent. Your total for Housing including all of these costs should not be more than 30 to 35 percent of your spendable income.

If you are reading this book, you may be one of the many who have more expenses than income. How can you make your budget balance? You have four choices.

1. You can continue the cycle of debt and despair.
2. You can earn more.
3. You can spend less and earn more.
4. You can spend less.

Don and Trina's Story

When I first met them, Don and Trina were a couple in their late twenties with two children ages eighteen months and three years. Don was a hard-working manufacturer's representative, a Choleric who was developing a case of workaholism. His career dominated his thoughts, leaving little time or energy for his family.

Trina was an elementary school teacher, a sunny Sanguine who quit work after the birth of their second child. Trina took over the management of the family finances, a task they had shared when both worked. But Trina could never keep track of the checkbook balance. Bills were misplaced and occasionally she was assessed a late charge when she forgot to pay a bill.

When Don and Trina filled out the Money Makeover Inventory it became apparent that they were spending thousands more than they earned each year, making up the shortfall by using their credit cards.

"In a few years you're going to be in bankruptcy if something isn't done quickly about your situation," I told them.

"We know we have to cut back our spending," Don admitted. "But we're not sure how much that will help."

I started going over the list of their bills.

"I just can't seem to get a handle on keeping track of our expenses," Trina said. "I'm not very good at budgeting."

I smiled at her and kept on punching numbers into my calculator. "You probably hate writing checks and dealing with this whole issue, am I right?"

"Is it that obvious?"

"You're like a lot of us," I assured her. "You seem like a happy Sanguine. A lot of Sanguines hate routine and forms. Numbers and arithmetic are your pet hates, I'll bet."

"Absolutely! I don't know whether the whole subject bores me or frightens me, but I can't seem to get organized."

"Let's start by simplifying the process. It may cost you a little each month, but in the long run it will save you money. I'm going to suggest that you team up with another personality type, one who enjoys working with numbers. It could be a relative, a friend or someone from church. Or you could hire a bookkeeping service."

They seemed relieved and agreed. Within a week they found a woman at their church who did bookkeeping in her home. For a small monthly charge she agreed to take over their bill-paying, record-keeping and checkbook balancing.

Trina stopped carrying a checkbook and limited herself to a weekly cash allowance. They cut up their credit cards and Don signed up for an automatic savings plan through his work.

With these initial changes in place, they set about the practical aspects of balancing their budget, paying off their bills, and starting on the road to prosperity.

Here is what Don and Trina's Debt/Income Statement looked like:

ANNUAL INCOME, after taxes	$30,372
MONTHLY INCOME, after taxes	2,531
Installment debts, balances	
Credit Card #1	1,750
Credit Card #2	2,250
Credit Card #3	1,508
Secured debts, balances	
Automobile	8,110
Living room furniture	1,802
TV and stereo	.463
Washer and dryer	.279
Other debts, balances	
Dept. store charge account, misc.	.490
TOTAL CONSUMER DEBT	**$16,652**
ALLOWABLE MAXIMUM DEBT (annual income x .20)	$6,074
Present consumer debt (Debt ÷ Present income)	55% OF SPENDABLE INCOME

Don and Trina had debt that totaled 55 percent of their spendable (after-tax) income. They needed to reduce their debt by $10,578 in order to bring it within limits that were prudent for their income. However, they wanted to be completely debt-free.

Their obligation on their automobile alone comprised 28 percent of their income. The original purchase price was $12,314, to be paid at 16 percent interest over forty-eight months. They had been paying on the car for twenty months; the balance was now $8,110.

Following is Don and Trina's Recapitulation of Expenses with starred (*) items for future planning:

Don and Trina—Monthly and Yearly Expenses

	Monthly	Yearly
TOTAL SPENDABLE INCOME	$2531	$30,372
Joyful Lifestyle Commitment		
Donations and Giving	$20	$240
Personal Gift Giving	40	480
Recreation, Entertainment, Vacations	60	720
Health, Beauty, etc.	40	480
Animals and Pets	0	0
Personal Allowances	0	0
Practical Lifestyle Commitment		
Housing Costs	$960	$11,520
Automobile Costs		
Payment	349	4,188
15,000 miles/year x $.30	375	4,500
Food	450	5,400
Clothing	80	960
Insurance	0	0
Health	25	300
Financial, Legal Assistance	0	0
Secure Lifestyle Commitment		
Present Credit Card Payments	$190	$2,280
Present Secured Debt Payments	105	1,260
Dept. Store Charge Accounts	22	264
Savings (Wage Security)	0	0
Savings (Home Security)	0	0
Savings (Auto Security)	0	0
Retirement/Pension	0	0
College Fund	0	0
Other: Accelerated Debt Reduction	0	0

TOTAL EXPENSES	$2,716	$32,592
DIFFERENCE BETWEEN INCOME AND EXPENSES	[185]	[2,220]

Starred (*) Items (in order of importance):

*Donations and Giving Increase	*80	*960
*Accelerated Debt Reduction	*91	*1,092
*Medical and Dental	*25	*300
*Life Insurance	*60	*720
*Renters Insurance	*15	*180
*Savings (Wage Security)	*100	*1,200
Total Starred (*) Items	*371	*4,452

With a spendable income of $30,372, their current spending was $2,220 over income each year. To make their budget balance, they would have to decrease spending by $185 per month and/or increase earnings by that amount, just to break even. In addition, they hoped to find ways to make room in their budget for at least three important starred (*) items.

What They Learned From the Money Makeover Inventory

Don and Trina had been living beyond their means and making up the difference by using their credit cards for clothing, gifts and entertainment. Not only did they have $16,652 in installment debts, they also had neglected or short-changed themselves in the following areas:

1. Giving. Their church giving had dropped considerably in the past couple of years, along with their attendance. They both expressed a desire to increase that portion of their budget.

2. Insurance. They wanted to take out additional

life insurance, in order to provide for Trina and the children if something happened to Don. They also wanted to take out renters insurance to protect against loss due to theft, fire or flood.

3. Savings. Like many young couples, they had no savings. At some point in the future, they wanted to save for a down payment on a home. They did not see how they could begin a meaningful savings program until their debts were paid off.

4. Health. They had been so short of money that they had neglected to get adequate dental check-ups.

5. Interest paid. Credit was costing them almost $3,000 a year in interest, so their first goal in terms of their Secure Lifestyle Commitment was to pay their debts as quickly as possible and not incur any new debt.

All of these items were starred (*), and totals indicated in the Money Makeover Inventory so that they could be worked into their spending plan sometime in the future. They listed the most pressing needs in the order of their importance, aiming to initially increase giving by $30, dental to $25, and pay off their debts as soon as possible.

The New Spending Plan

They decided they did not want Trina to go to work for a least three or four years because their children were still very young. Also, they agreed that it was important for Don to have sufficient time with Trina and the children. His getting a second job was to be only a last resort if all other solutions failed. They talked together over the next several weeks as they wrestled with the figures. Gradually, choices became clear to them.

Let's take a look at Don and Trina's primary goals:

Joyful Lifestyle Commitment #1: Increase Giving

The first item of consideration was Don and Trina's goal of achieving a giving level of $100 per month. Under their present budget they were giving $20 per month. They planned to immediately start giving an additional $30 per month, eventually increasing to their goal of $100.

Practical Lifestyle Commitment #1: Provide for Dental Care

One of the items they had been ignoring was adequate dental care. Because they had so many other bills, they had been putting off getting their regular checkups for themselves and the children. Their ultimate goal was to budget $50 per month for medical expenses to supplement their health insurance coverage. For the time being, though, they wanted to be able to immediately budget $25 for dental care.

Secure Lifestyle Commitment #1: Debt Retirement

One of Don and Trina's greatest concerns was their excessive load of debt which amounted to 55 percent of their annual spendable income. The car loan would be paid off in twenty-eight more months.

Don and Trina wanted to be completely debt-free in twenty-eight months—by the time they made their last car payment. Their other installment debts, not including the car, totalled $8,542. If they added $91 more per month to their payments, they could pay off all their other debts within twenty-eight months.

In order to make their plan work they would have to come up with a total of $331 per month (the $185 per month they were already "in the red" plus $91 to apply toward accelerated debt reduction and $55 for the other two important starred (*) items they had selected as most pressing). Their goal was to do this without Trina's having to work away from home.

How could they possibly come up with $331 more per month?

Don and Trina did this by making a series of decisions. This process involved going through the Money Makeover Inventory page by page and reviewing past spending, finding ways to cut back on present spending or defer other categories until all debts were paid.

Don and Trina's Decisions

Don and Trina's primary goals were:

1. Increase giving immediately to $50 per month ($30 increase) and eventually to $100.

2. Get debt-free in twenty-eight months.

3. Provide for dental care ($25).

The intermediate steps they identified as necessary to achieve their primary goals were as follows:

1. Continue making regular payments on the automobile, paying it off in twenty-eight months.

2. Pay off all other installment debt within the same twenty-eight months (an increase of $91 per month).

3. Not make any further credit purchases.

4. Reduce spending to balance spending with income. Work on specific ways to accomplish this, using the figures entered in the Money Makeover Inventory.

Intermediate step #4 was broken down into specific steps, as follows:

1. They decided that, for the next twenty-eight months, they would not buy any clothes except necessary clothing for the kids; that they would buy these whenever possible at thrift stores or bargain basements; that they would ask grandparents to give clothing instead of toys for gifts. Net estimated monthly saving: $60.

2. Trina did a comparison study of bulk buying and savings to be made by buying less processed foods ($20), cutting out desserts, junk foods and soft drinks ($15), and shopping at discount houses ($35) for cleaning supplies, paper goods, etc. Net monthly saving: $70.

3. By limiting gift giving and making homemade gifts, they reduced their gift expenses to $20 per month. They decided that for their gifts to each other for their anniversary and Christmas, they would prefer to give each other the gift of being debt-free. Net monthly saving: $20.

4. Even though they enjoyed their membership at the local gym, they agreed they would get nearly the same benefits and quality time together by taking up jogging. Net monthly saving: $20.

Total net saving: $170 per month.

Since their goal was $331 including the three additional starred (*) items they had added to their decision list, they still needed another $161 per month in order to reach their three primary goals. Once again they made a pass at the figures, looking for ways to reduce spending. They had saved in just about every area they could think of except one—their transportation expenses.*

After going over his figures, Don decided to car pool to work for $10 per week ($43 per month). That cut his car mileage and maintenance expenses by two-thirds . . . from 15,000 annual miles to 5,000. This lowered his transportation costs from $375 per month ($4,500 per year) to $125 per month ($1,500 per year). His net saving was $250 per month. (Some insurance companies also lower insurance rates for drivers who carpool, which would effect additional savings.)

The savings they had made broke down as follows:

Goal = $331

Miscellaneous reductions in spending	$170
Savings effected by carpooling	250
Total Savings	420
Amount Over Goal	89

When Don and Trina started taking a hard look at their spending, they found they could exceed their original goal. They went back to their starred (*) items list, and increased their giving another $50 to reach their goal of $100 and set aside $39 for life insurance.

Their new spending plan looked like this:

Don and Trina's New Spending Plan

	Monthly	Yearly
Joyful Lifestyle Commitment		
Donations and Giving	$100	$1,200
Personal Gift Giving	20	240

* As part of Don and Trina's five-year plan, they decided that they wanted to pay cash for their next car, rather than incurring new debt. They decided they would establish a car fund as part of that goal. In the next chapter, we will show you how they accomplished their goal of paying cash for their next car.

Recreation, Entertainment, Vacations	60	720
Health, Beauty, etc.	20	240
Animals and Pets	0	0
Personal Allowances	0	0

Practical Lifestyle Commitment

Housing Costs	$960	$11,520
Automobile Costs		
Payments	349	4,188
Other: 5,000 miles/$.30	125	1,500
Food	380	4,560
Clothing	20	240
Insurance	39	468
Health	50	600
Financial, Legal Assistance	0	0

Secure Lifestyle Commitment

Present Credit Card Payments	$190	$2,280
Present Secured Debt Payments	105	1,260
Dept. Store Charge Accounts	22	264
Savings (Wage Security)	0	0
Savings (Home Security)	0	0
Savings (Auto Security)	0	0
Retirement/Pension	0	0
College Fund	0	0
Other: Accelerated Debt Reduction	91	1,092
GRAND TOTALS	**2,531**	**30,372**
Difference	**0**	**0**

Remaining Starred (*) Items (in order of importance)

*Life Insurance	$11	$132
*Renters Insurance	15	180
*Savings (Wage Security)	100	1,200
Total (*) Items:	126	1,512

Don and Trina could have taken longer to pay off their debts. Trina could have taken an outside job to earn more money. Don could have looked for a higher-paying position. There are many different ways they could have chosen to solve their problem and reach their goal. The important thing is not how they chose to do it, but that they *did* do it.

Your Decisions

Begin to go over your expenses based on the Recapitulation of Expenses from the Money Makeover Inventory. Answer these questions:

1. How much do you have to cut back spending (or increase earning) in order to bring your expenses in line with your income?

Our total annual expenses: ____

Our total annual income: ____

Difference (+ or -): ____

2. What decisions can you make starting today, to begin making that process happen?

3. Using the blank Decision List at the end of this chapter, item by item, go down the list of items and start now to make the small decisions that will add up to big savings.

In the next chapter, we'll explore how Don and Trina made their new spending plan work on a daily basis, and through that process, show you how you can too.

$ $ $

Suggestions for Personal and Group Study

Individuals

1. Study the following list. How many of these savings can you put into place in your budget?

   - Sell some luxury or nonessential assets such as boat, extra car, vacation lot
   - Move in temporarily with relatives
   - Take extra part-time job
   - Quit spa and take up jogging
   - Give up desserts
   - Quit smoking
   - Switch from soft drinks to tap water
   - Join car pool
   - Turn down thermostat
   - Cut down on nonessential use of electricity: cut TV watching to four hours per week, shut off air conditioner, turn off lights when you leave a room
   - Shop at thrift stores, second-hand stores for good used clothing
   - Buy groceries in bulk at discount stores
   - Cut down on use of processed foods; make wise use of leftovers, cut out junk food
   - Make inexpensive gifts
   - For large families, have each person draw a name for adults at Christmas
   - Move to smaller, cheaper home
   - Move to location where rents are lower
   - If you own a home, consider buying a duplex so

that rental income can help pay mortgage

2. Describe some additional savings you can put into place:

Groups

1. Have the group discuss ways they have found of cutting back spending.
2. After you have figured out which categories you will cut back, and/or how you can increase your income to make your income and expenses balance, recap the figures to the Decision List on the following pages.

Decision List

We need to reduce our spending by $________ per year/ $__________ per month. We made our decisions on: __________________ (date)

	Description of Decisions	Amount Saved Per Month
Joyful Living Commitment		
Donations	____________________	________
and	____________________	________
Giving	____________________	________
Personal	____________________	________
Gift	____________________	________
Giving	____________________	________
Recreation,	____________________	________
Entertain-	____________________	________
ment	____________________	________
Personal	____________________	________
Health,	____________________	________
Beauty, etc.	____________________	________
Pets	____________________	________
	____________________	________
	____________________	________
Personal	____________________	________
Allowances	____________________	________
	____________________	________
Subtotal		________
Practical Living Commitment		
Housing	____________________	________
Costs	____________________	________
	____________________	________

Automobile	________________	________
	________________	________
	________________	________
Food	________________	________
	________________	________
	________________	________
Clothing	________________	________
	________________	________
	________________	________
Insurance	________________	________
	________________	________
	________________	________
Subtotal		________
TOTAL THAT WE CAN SAVE		________

How Long Will It Take to Pay Off Your Installment Debts?

Monthly Payment You Will Need to Make and Number of Years

You Owe	One Year	Two Years	Three Years	Four Years	Five Years	Six Years	Seven Years	Eight Years	Nine Years	Ten Years	Eleven Years	Twelve Years
5000	463	254	186	152	132	120	111	105	100	97	94	92
6000	556	305	223	183	159	144	133	126	120	116	113	110
7000	648	356	260	213	185	168	155	147	140	135	132	129
8000	741	407	297	243	212	192	178	168	160	155	150	147
9000	834	458	334	274	238	216	200	189	180	174	169	165
10,000	926	509	372	304	265	240	222	210	200	193	188	184
11,000	1019	560	409	335	292	263	244	230	220	213	207	202
12,000	1112	611	446	365	318	287	266	251	240	232	225	220
13,000	1204	662	483	396	344	311	289	272	260	251	244	239
14,000	1297	713	520	426	371	335	311	293	280	271	263	257
15,000	1390	763	557	456	397	359	333	314	300	290	282	276
20,000	1853	1018	743	609	530	479	444	419	401	387	376	367
25,000	2316	1272	929	761	662	599	555	524	501	483	470	459
30,000	2779	1527	1115	913	795	719	666	629	601	580	564	551

This chart is calculated at 20 percent annual interest rate. If you want exact figures based on the rate of interest you are paying on your obligations, go to the bookstore or library and get a book containing tables of amortization schedules such as *Compound Interest Tables* by Michael Sherman, *The Consumer's Amortization Guide* by Dugan Publishers or *Interest Amortization Tables* by Jack C. Estes

8

Putting Your Ideas Into Action

Step 7: Design a plan consistent with your personality.

Don't give up whatever you're trying to do—
especially if you're convinced that you're botching it up.
Giving up reinforces a sense of incompetence,
going on gives you a commitment to success.
—George Weinberg

Get up! Pick up your mat and walk (John 5:8, NIV).

"I like money. It's just that I hate keeping track of it," one of my clients told me.

She's like most of us. We like to spend, but we hate to be held accountable for our spending, even when we are only holding ourselves accountable.

But money must be managed. *Management* is the price we pay to gain security, financial freedom and prosperity.

There is good news, however. The process of money management need not be burdensome. I even have people tell me, after working the Money Makeover for a few months, that they enjoy the program. They find out that it feels good to get control over their lives.

There is no universal bookkeeping system that is perfect for everyone. In the Money Makeover you don't have to use the same method as your accountant, your next-door neighbor or your brother. You can choose a system that fits your personality, your lifestyle and your goals.

Woody Allen says, "Eighty percent of success is showing up." Whatever system you choose, whether it is simple or complex, you must at least show up—you must take charge and follow through.

An Wang, the founder of Wang Laboratories, said that "Success is more a function of consistent common sense than it is of genius." On The Money Makeover you will design your own money management system, using your own good common sense. With consistent practice, you will find your finances changing dramatically within just a few months and with relative ease because the system is one that uniquely suits *you.*

Whatever the process you adopt, it shouldn't become another form of slavery for you. If the system you use frees you from the worry, indecision and fear that now surrounds money issues, then it is probably right for you. This leads us to

Step 7:
Design a plan consistent with your personality.

The modules of the Money Makeover system are interchangeable, just like the components you might use to put together a stereo system or landscaping design. You can use almost any combination of the following elements to devise your own personalized money management system.

Cash Envelope

Obtain some sturdy 5" x 8" or 9" x 12" manila envelopes (the kinds with brass clasps) from the stationery

Spending Plan Envelopes

5"x 8" envelopes marked as follows: **Food, Household, Gifts, Recreation, Entertainment.** Allow **Personal Allowance** envelopes for each member of the household.

Matthew's PERSONAL ALLOWANCE
$ ____ per month

Clothes
Haircuts
Hobbies
School lunches
Prom
Gifts for friends

HOUSEHOLD
$ ____ per month

Cleaning supplies
Light bulbs
Batteries
Housekeeper
Towels
Small appliances
Appliance repairs
Gardening supplies

ENTERTAINMENT
$ ____ per month

Company dinners
Holidays
Movies
Video rentals

GIFTS
$ ____ per month

LIST
- Grandma
- Grandpa
- Mother
- Father
- Matthew
- Jessica
- Stephen

store. Label the envelopes: *Food, Household, Gifts, Recreation, Entertainment, Personal Allowances* (one envelope for each family member), *Clothing*, and any other categories you choose. Under the label on each envelope, describe the specific types of expenses which are covered by that category so that later on there will be no confusion or argument about how the money is to be spent.

The basic rule is this: You can spend the money in the envelope; when it is gone you must stop spending. You cannot borrow money from another envelope. That's cheating.

If you have planned $30 a month for gifts and you get paid twice a month, you will put $15 into the Gifts envelope each pay period. The money in the envelope is to be used only for gifts.

If you know that in six months you have a big holiday to plan for, you can keep adding to the envelope each payday until you have accumulated the amount needed.

Some people keep their envelopes in their Budget Box, but if you are afraid of burglars, you can keep your money anywhere you think it will be safe. I had one lady tell me she kept her money in the back of the freezer in frozen fruit containers (empty, I presume). This demonstrates that there are an infinite variety of methods you can use, but I am not sure your money should be kept on ice.

Our dear friend Jim Moon proposes what I think is a much better solution. Jim is a highly successful businessman who was able to retire in his forties. He had to overcome many childhood struggles to become the highly accomplished person he is today. A turning point for him, he says, came about when he bought a safe in which to keep his cash and valuables. At that time he was just beginning to understand the financial principles which eventually brought him his fortune. The seemingly insignificant act of locking away his hard-earned money had an important effect on his attitudes. He says that from that time on he began to take his earnings more seriously.

You should view your money as important. If you

can afford one, a safe may be a good investment and a powerful psychological tool in your program to achieve financial liberation.

Travelers' Checks

If you hate to keep cash in the envelopes, buy travelers' checks at the bank. You can keep these in your freezer or, even better, buy a safe as my friend Jim did.

Checkbook

A checkbook is a convenient way to pay for things without carrying around cash. It can also be a veritable pain, simply because it involves little boxes and squares (forms again!), a balance that never seems to match the bank statement, worries over writing bounced checks and marital disputes.

It would be wonderful if you would never make a mistake in your checkbook. But if you're like me, it will happen occasionally. We do it, that's all. If we are Sanguine or Choleric, we do it fairly regularly. For Cholerics, our goal is to have enough money in the bank so we will never again have to worry if a check will clear. We don't care about the balance, most of the time. We don't want to know the exact figures, we just want to hurry up and write a check and get whatever it is we want.

Not everyone thinks that checkbooks are devices of torture. Some people actually like balancing them, and do very well at it. For some people a checkbook, with or without a ledger (see below), is a wonderfully convenient form of making purchases. They like writing down the little numbers, doing all the adding and subtracting, and writing in the name of the person who is getting the check. For others, a checking account is a constant worry. They don't like to think about such things.

Throughout Yuppiedom (and DINKdom* too, for that matter), it is worse than a sin to admit you hate checking accounts. It is an admission that you are either a failure or simply not "with it," which is almost the same thing. So people keep checking accounts because they think it is expected of them and because everyone else is doing it.

Did you know it is quite possible to get along in life without a checking account? It is not only possible, it is permissible.

My late sister-in-law was a world-famous movie actress, the star of *The Moon Is Blue.* At the height of her career she had no checking account. Was she too poor and ignorant to have one? No, she was too successful and smart.

Jeff is one of my former clients who, after a divorce, found himself facing bankruptcy. After he regained control of his finances, he found himself a wonderful young lady who helps him stay on a cash-only system. Jeff says he doesn't miss not having a checking account. "When the money is spent, we just don't spend until the money is there." Jeff and Tammi are building a strong financial future without the use of a checking account or credit cards. They use the bank to save money, not spend it. As their savings grow, their confidence does, too.

So the first thing you can acknowledge is that a checking account is optional.

Frequently the reason a checking account becomes such a chore is that there are dozens of checks we have to write each month to pay charge accounts and credit cards. When all your bills are paid off, and you only have to pay such things as rent, utilities, and so on, you may find that a checking account is not nearly so menacing.

* DINK is an acronym used by contemporary sociologists and economists to indicate couples with "Double Income, No Kids."

You will have fewer bills to pay each month; you may even find balancing your account a welcome challenge.

Do you absolutely hate and fear the prospect of balancing your bank statement? In Appendix A, I give you some hints on how to cope with this nuisance.

Written Ledger

Ledgers are available at any stationery store and anyone can learn to use one. The ledger should be set up to include a daily journal which shows in chronological order what you earn and what you spend. There should be separate sections for expenses such as Housing, Utilities, and so forth.

If you are going to keep your own checkbook, I advise that you have a large business-type checkbook that carries three checks to a page. You can order ledger sheets that are included as part of the checkbook. There are many good systems available through your bank. There is a "one-write" system of bookkeeping that enters figures to the ledger automatically as you hand-write the check. There are business-size checks that are available with either one or two carbonless copies. For instance, when you write a check to the doctor, you might want to put one copy of the check into the medical folder in your Budget Box, and leave the other copy in the checkbook. In this way you have your spending organized by subject (Budget Box folder) and by date (checkbook).

Money Orders

If you hate the very idea of a checking account, money orders can free you from having to reconcile your bank statement. You won't have to worry about writing a bad check. Take your paycheck to the bank with your bills, some stamps and envelopes, and purchase money orders for all your bills. Have the teller give you just enough cash for the week's expenses, and put the rest in savings. On the way home from the bank, mail the bills. Your accounting worries are over.

I don't advise you to buy money orders at convenience stores or grocery stores because a number of these private companies have gone bankrupt, leaving a trail of bounced money orders. A money order that you purchase from the bank is much safer.

It is important to get the kind of money order that provides you a duplicate, so you can have a record of your payment to keep in your Budget Box.

Of course, never, ever pay bills by sending cash through the mail.

Automatic Savings

Once you have your debts reduced to the point where you have money left over after necessary expenses, this automatic system enables you to save without effort. Some banks offer this service. You can authorize the bank to withdraw a certain sum from your checking account every month on a certain date and transfer it to savings. You may be able to sign up with a credit union through your employer to have a sum taken from your paycheck and deposited to savings.

Credit Card

Some of you (you know who you are) are sufficiently disciplined to be able to carry a credit card for specific expenditures for convenience, such as a gasoline credit card which is paid off every thirty days. A credit card also may be useful in the case of a college student who is living away from home and has a personal allowance. Of course, this only works if the student is responsible.

The thirty-day credit account is a convenient way of

handling certain types of expenses. In general, it does not encourage debting as long as the credit card charges are paid in full at the end of every thirty days.

However, some surveys indicate that when you use a credit card you spend 30 percent or more than if you were paying cash. Recently, two national fast-food chains introduced credit cards at selected restaurants to test-market their feasibility. They found that people would pay twice as much for a meal when they could charge it!

Beware of credit cards.

Outside Bookkeeper

I've already mentioned the benefits of having someone take care of your bookkeeping for you. This may be a person you live with, a friend, someone at church, or a professional service. Your bookkeeper is one to whom you will explain your budget goals and your five-year plan.

The services that will be provided should be clearly understood (if possible, in writing) by all parties. Do not delegate the task of actually signing checks to anyone other than your spouse, unless your bookkeeper is a person in whom you have absolute, utter, unshakable confidence and trust. Your bookkeeper may provide any or all of the following services:

1. Receive your bills, either from you or directly from the creditor.
2. Make out checks and pay the bills on time.
3. Receive your paycheck and deposit it in the bank.
4. Maintain a running bank balance so you can know at all times how much you have in the bank.
5. Figure out a cash allowance or living allotment

and give you that money to live on during each pay period, and keep the rest of your money in the bank so it can be available for bills, savings, etc.

6. Provide you a monthly or quarterly statement of your finances.

7. Alert you to upcoming periodic expenses.

8. Help you in preparing your taxes by keeping track of tax deductible expenses.

Personal Allowances

For personal allowances, use a separate envelope for each person in the family, writing that person's name clearly on the front. Then describe in detail the expenses the person should pay out of the allowance. For example, Dad might pay for his haircuts, chewing gum, dry cleaning and his own clothing. Mom might use her allowance to pay for beauty shop, magazines, gym membership and clothing.

It may take several weeks for a family to decide how much the personal allowances should be and what should be paid from them. This is an important part of financial planning that should not be ignored. Each person should feel they have at least a small amount of money over which they have control.

Computer

No matter what your personality type, you may find a computer makes money management chores pleasant, once you find the right software. My personal belief is that the perfect computer for Sanguines, Cholerics and Phlegmatics is the MacIntosh, using any of the simple-to-use software such as Quicken™ or Dollars & Sense™. But there are also other brands of computers on the market that are easy to use, including inexpensive IBM clones. If you are new to computers, this is not the time to go out and spend thousands of dollars on an untried system. Try one out first, perhaps by using a friend's unit. When you get ready to buy, check out your newspaper or local computer swap meet, where you can get a good buy on used equipment. I have purchased almost-new equipment that was still under factory warranty for about half price, and have been very happy with the result. Some computer stores will let you rent or try out their systems before you make a purchase.

I have found the computer fun to use, and anyone can learn to operate the bookkeeping programs I have just mentioned with a couple of hours of practice. If you have trouble with numbers, you may find that a computer will forever change your view of arithmetic. I have clients who can't wait to get home at night to play with their computers—people who, formerly, couldn't bear to look at a column of figures.

You can indicate to the computer the amount you want to budget in each category of your spending plan, and it can then tell you how close your spending is to your budget. My Macintosh is my resident Melancholy. It never lies to me, and as long as I give it the information I have at my disposal, it keeps me informed and organized in spite of myself.

Try this system if you are a Sanguine married to another Sanguine: Take turns keying in the data and then discuss the results the computer is giving you. There is something marvelously impersonal about the computer as a partner in your financial management program.

Adopt Your Own "Track"

Now that you have identified some essential components, it is time to examine ways you can put these separate pieces together to form your own money management system. Following are five different tracks you can choose from. Or design your own, choosing the individual elements in a combination that will work for you.

Track A: The Cash Envelope/Automated Savings/ Money Order Method

- payroll deduction savings
- cash for daily expenditures
- money orders for bills

This system is useful for Phlegmatics and Sanguines because it is simple, flexible and requires very little discipline. You only need to make one trip to the bank to buy money orders to pay bills and get cash for the week's living expenses. Since taking out cash is contemporaneous with the act of paying bills, you are receiving at the same time that you are paying. This makes it easier to keep current with obligations. Track A works well for a single person or a small family with few obligations and a relatively simple lifestyle.

Track B: The Checkbook/Automated Savings/ Cash Envelope Method

- bank savings
- checks to pay bills
- cash envelopes for living expenses

In Track B, the checkbook can be managed by you, your spouse or an outside bookkeeper. Automated savings can be accomplished either through a payroll deduction plan or through your bank if it offers this service. This system is adaptable to the Sanguine or Choleric who wants to maintain some control and accountability over expenditures, perhaps by utilizing a ledger or one-write system in conjunction with the checkbook.

Everything other than monthly payments is organized in cash envelopes. This cuts down on bookkeeping. In order to keep track of the money that is in the envelopes, all you have to do is be able to count. This appeals to the Sanguine's love of simplicity and the Choleric's love of short-cuts (getting things done *now*).

Track C: The Bookkeeping Service/Credit Card/ Cash Envelope Method

- credit cards limited to specific expenses
- checkbook for recurring bills maintained by bookkeeper
- cash envelopes for small expenditures
- savings, automated or not

This system can be partially delegated to a business manager or bookkeeping service, who should be given a copy of your Spending Plan, so you can be notified when you are getting close to your spending limits in each category. The bookkeeping service can balance your checking account, give you a monthly or quarterly statement of how you are doing, and prepare checks for your signature to pay your bills. This system works for a larger family, especially where a wage-earner travels extensively.

The Choleric and the Sanguine will find this system adaptable to their personalities since it gives them some control. It also relieves them of tedious detail, which they both hate—and the need for self-discipline, which is sometimes in short supply.

Track D: The Checkbook/Written Ledger/ Cash Personal Allowance Method

- checkbook for almost every expense

- written ledgers
- cash to individuals as personal allowances

The Melancholy will find this a workable and convenient system, and will probably feel comfortable taking care of all aspects of it, including entering expenditures into a ledger for purposes of keeping track of spending in each category.

The only cash in this system is that which is handed out for personal allowances. Make sure every member of the family knows exactly which expenses are expected to be paid from the individual's allowance.

Track E: The Checkbook/Computer Backup Method

- checkbook for bills
- cash envelopes for incidentals and allowances
- computer to keep track of spending

A computer can assist in assigning budget categories, writing checks and reconciling the bank account. Savings may be automated if you wish. Cash envelopes are still a handy way of keeping track of smaller household expenditures and personal allowances.

The computer can be used to automatically print out checks for each month's recurring obligations such as mortgage payments. It can track items with tax implications such as medical expenses. Best of all, it can play games with you when you're finished with your budget!

Balancing the Budget

Now that you have designed your own money-management system, you are ready to set up your own Spending Plan. Using the Inventory and the Recapitulation of Expenses as a guide, transfer the totals from each main category into the Spending Plan on page 166. As a review, here is how the expenses should be grouped together:

Donations and Giving. Includes tithes, offerings, charitable donations and miscellaneous charitable giving.

Recreation, Entertainment, Vacations. Includes holiday gatherings, Christmas and Easter decorations, movies, video rentals, vacations, weekend trips, dining out and all costs for babysitters associated with such events.

Housing. Includes all costs associated with shelter: rent or mortgage payments, utilities, homeowner's insurance, house maintenance, furniture, repairs, cleaning, gardening, painting and property taxes.

Clothing. Includes purchase, repair, laundry and cleaning.

Auto. Includes all costs associated with operation of any given vehicle: payment, insurance, taxes, registration, car washes, maintenance, repairs, gasoline and oil.

Health. Medical, dental costs, prescriptions, orthodontist and health insurance.

Food. Grocery items, except for guests, which is included under Recreation.

Insurance. Life insurance, disability insurance, and any other insurance not included in Housing, Auto and Health.

Using the information from your Recapitulation of Expenses (pages 75 to 77) and your Decision List (pages 148 and 149), figure out what your new monthly spending plan will be based on the changes you have decided to make (see the next page). In the first column, **Recap Amount**, write down the *monthly* totals from your Recapitulation of Expenses forms. In the next column, **Decision Amount**, indicate how much you decided to increase or decrease your spending in each category, taking the information from your Decision List.

For example, if your personal gift-giving expense was $80 on your Recapitulation of Expenses, you would write down $80 in the Recap Amount column. If your Decision List shows you decided to cut your gift-giving budget by $20, you would write -$20 in the Decision Amount column and subtract that amount from your Recap Amount, entering $60 in the New Plan column.

You may find it necessary to go through your Recapitulation of Expenses and Decision List several times before you reach the point where your expenses are no more than your income. Remember that even small cuts in spending will eventually yield dramatic results, as you saw in the example of Don and Trina in chapter 7.

Your New Monthly Spending Plan

	Recap Amount	Decision Amount (+/-)	New Plan
Joyful Lifestyle Commitment			
Donations and Giving	____	____	____
Personal Gift Giving	____	____	____
Recreation, Vacations, Entertainment	____	____	____
Personal Health, Beauty, etc.	____	____	____
Animals and Pets	____	____	____
SUBTOTAL	____	____	____
Practical Lifestyle Commitment			
Housing Costs	____	____	____
Automobile	____	____	____
Food	____	____	____

Clothing	____	____	____
Insurance	____	____	____
Health	____	____	____
Financial, Legal Assistance	____	____	____
SUBTOTAL	____	____	____

Secure Lifestyle Commitment

Credit Card Debt Reduction	____	____	____
Secured Debt Reduction	____	____	____
Other Misc. Debt Reduction	____	____	____
Savings (Wage Security)	____	____	____
Savings (Home Security)	____	____	____
Savings (Auto Security)	____	____	____
Retirement, Pension	____	____	____
College Fund	____	____	____
Other	____	____	____
SUBTOTAL	____	____	____
GRAND TOTALS	____	____	____

Unplanned but Necessary or Desirable (in order of importance)
* items:

____________	____	____	____
____________	____	____	____
____________	____	____	____
____________	____	____	____
TOTAL (*) Items:	____	____	____

Starred (*) Categories

Go back to your list of starred (*) items. Can any of these be included in your Spending Plan at this time? If your starred (*) items are not essential, you can postpone them as Don and Trina did, until such time as you can comfortably afford to include one or more of them in your budget. In the meantime, having a list of these items is a reminder of your goals.

However, if you have starred items that are vital, you must decide how you can find room for these in your budget. For instance, if you do not now have car insurance, you must decrease spending in another area in order to make an allowance for this necessary expense.

Balancing the Triad

Are you spending too much in one category and too little in another? Rather than worry about what percentage of your income you should be spending on clothing or food or entertainment, try to emphasize over-all balance between the three areas of spending: Joyful, Practical and Secure.

Installment debts are listed under the Secure Lifestyle because your first investment goal should be to pay off your debts. The banks are charging you up to 20 percent interest, sometimes more, for the privilege of using your credit cards. By paying these obligations off ahead of schedule, you will in effect be earning a guaranteed rate of return of 20 percent (or whatever they are charging you) on your money.

Some people will advise you to "pay yourself first," that is, start a savings account even while you are using credit or before you have your debts paid to a reasonable level. If you are relying on credit and trying to save, you are fooling yourself. It does not make sense to put money in the bank earning 6 percent while you are still using credit cards that are costing you 20 percent for your purchases. Pay your debts off or reduce them until they are no more than 20 percent of your annual spendable income. Then start a savings program in earnest.

How much should you be spending in each of the three main groups? While no hard-and-fast rules apply (and I think that each family's needs vary so greatly that rules are useless), you might aim for approximately 20 percent for Joyful Lifestyle, perhaps 50 to 70 percent for Practical Lifestyle, and 10 to 30 percent for Secure Lifestyle.

Keep your Decisions List in a permanent and visible location where you can review it daily, and remind yourself of the decisions you have made. As you review the list, ask yourself these questions:

1. Am I sticking to my decisions to save in each area?

2. Could I save even more in any category?

Credit Counseling

What if your debts are so far out of control that budgeting doesn't begin to reach the problem? If you are being hounded by creditors and threatened with lawsuits, you may benefit by consulting with a credit counselor. Sometimes this service is free; other times there is a nominal charge. There are credit counseling services in many communities which are funded by local business organizations who make voluntary contributions to support this worthwhile work.

The credit counselor will review your expenses and debts and help you structure a payment plan. He will give you a budget that eliminates frills such as recreation, entertainment and gifts. Then the counselor will get in touch with your creditors to propose a repayment schedule. Out of each paycheck you will pay the credit counselor a pre-determined amount, and he will use this money to pay your debts.

To find out the name and address of a credit counseling service in your community, check your local telephone directory. You can also contact the National Foundation for Consumer Credit, Inc., 8701 Georgia Avenue, Silver Springs, MD 10901, (301) 589-5600.

Help for Compulsive Spenders

"My spending is out of control, and I am afraid my problem can't be solved through reason, budgets and willpower. I think my overspending is a compulsive, driving force beyond my ability to manage."

If that describes the nature of your debting problem there is help in the form of a twelve-step program patterned after Alcoholics Anonymous. The organization is called Debtors Anonymous and it has chapters in many metropolitan areas.

The value of this group is that others with similar struggles can share with you their support, caring and advice. What if there is no Debtors Anonymous group in your community? Think of starting one, perhaps using an available room one evening a week at your local library or church. You can run an ad in the church bulletin or local newspaper and invite others with a similar problem to join you in the process of recovery.

For information on available chapters, or how to start your own group, send a stamped, self-addressed envelope to Debtors Anonymous, General Services Board, P. O. Box 20322, New York, NY 10025-9992; (212) 642-8220.

If you don't have access to a support group, there are many things you can do on your own to break yourself of the overspending habit.

1. Never carry credit cards. Some of us can exercise enough restraint to carry a gasoline credit card, of the type that is paid in full every month. Others may carry one other card, just for extreme emergencies.

2. Don't carry a checkbook with you. Carry $20 or so in emergency spending money, just to cover the day's contingencies. See #3 below.

3. For home use, get a large professional-type checkbook with business-size checks, three to a page, with the large stub at the left side for writing in details. The advantage of this is, of course, similar to #1. If you have to make a trip to the store, you remove only one check. (Remember to bring the receipt home with you and fill in the check stub. Or, if you have the type of checks that produce one or two carbonless copies, you can rip out the check and one copy so you will have a reproduction of the actual check.)

4. Follow the $20/24 system. This is a wait-and-think-it-over system that can be used to regulate your own personal allowance spending as well as family spending. Basically it involves determining that you will put off any purchase of $20 for at least twenty-four hours. If the purchase is $40, you must wait forty-eight hours (two days). If the purchase is $60, you will wait three days, and so on. After a day or two of waiting, that solar powered coffee maker may not seem quite so necessary after all.

5. Pray as you go. Ask the Lord's blessing before every purchase. Our checkbooks reveal our priorities, so we should ask His guidance before we buy. Ask yourself these questions:

a. Will this purchase honor God?

b. Is it in line with my Five-Year Plan?

c. Does this purchase further God's will in my life?

d. Is it in keeping with existing financial commitments?

If the answer to any of these questions is negative, let God have the veto power. This is most emphatically true if the contemplated purchase involves use of credit. As J. André Weisbrod says:

> But what is the greater demonstration of faith? Is it to commit and spend before God has provided, presuming upon His kindness to bail us out, or to pray and wait on Him to provide, only moving ahead as He verifies our desires and decisions with His provision? If God is big enough to bail us out when we irresponsibly go into debt, is He not big enough to provide up front?[1]

I call this strategy the "Pray as You Go, Pay as You Go" system of personal finance. People who have tried it tell me it works better than any other method they have used. Try it and see if you agree.

Tithing: The Glue That Holds It All Together

Tithing is a very personal and sometimes touchy subject. Some people become defensive when the issue is raised. They don't know where they would get that "extra" 10 percent, since they are already having problems paying their bills. And maybe they don't really know if they want to give that 10 percent anyway. Further, some churches stress tithing and others do not, so there is little general agreement.

I have never felt that it does any good to rebuke or push people into tithing before they are ready.

> Let everyone give as his heart tells him, neither grudgingly nor under compulsion, for God loves the man who gives cheerfully (2 Corinthians 9:7, Phillips).

Some ministers believe that the commitment to tithe is a by-product of a healthy and growing relationship with God. Many people attest to the increased blessings, material and spiritual, that flow from a decision to give the Lord the firstfruits of their wealth.

Chuck Snyder, author of *I Prayed for Patience and Other Horror Stories,* puts it this way:

> We decided to give 11 percent rather than 10 percent because we have so much more in Christ than the Jewish people had in the Law. Some people treat tithing as just another obligation, and leave it until near the end of their check writing just to make sure they have enough for the electricity, rent and other bills. If they don't have enough money that month, they may delay God's portion, knowing He is patient and won't zap them with lightning—but the landlord might!
>
> Barb and I suggest making out God's check FIRST. When we started doing this we were amazed. He helped us make our 89 percent go much further than the 100 percent did.[2]

If you are new to the idea of tithing and have not yet tried it, why not start out with a commitment to give a particular percent of your income? Once you make a pledge, be faithful in following through.

As you continue in careful stewardship, keep on praying about the way God wants you to use the money He has loaned you. It is my experience that as you do so, you will find that He will not only pour out an increasing blessing upon you—He will both motivate and empower you to give more and more as He multiplies your resources.

> He will open to you His wonderful treasury of rain in the heavens, to give you fine crops every season. He will bless everything you do; and you shall lend to many nations, but shall not borrow from them (Deuteronomy 28:12, TLB).

Are you at that place in your personal walk with God where you are wondering if there could be more to faith? Is the Lord calling you to greater reliance upon Him? It may be time to prayerfully re-examine your attitude toward tithing.

Perhaps you want to find ways to make giving, as well as spending and saving, a part of your permanent financial plan. A five-year plan is the key to translating dreams into reality. In the next chapter you and I will work together to

- identify your dreams
- lock them in place
- build a framework for achieving them

Giving as well as receiving will play a large part in the success of the next phase of your Money Makeover. Let's find out how.

$ $ $

Suggestions for Personal and Group Study

Individuals

Through the process of completing this chapter you have made decisions about the following. Check off the individual elements you have decided will work best for you and your family.

1. Where you will keep your records.
   - The Budget Box
2. How to keep track of how much money you have and spend.
   - cash envelopes
   - checkbook
   - outside bookkeeper
   - written ledger
   - computer
3. How to pay bills.
   - check
   - money order
   - travelers' checks
   - cash
   - delegate to outside bookkeeper
4. What to do about small purchases.
   - covered by personal allowances
   - cash envelopes
5. Which Track did you select?
   - Track A
   - Track B
   - Track C
   - Track D
   - Other:
6. Is your Budget Box completed?
7. Is it where you can use it daily?

8. What additional items do you need to purchase or what tasks do you need to perform to complete your Budget Box? List them below and beside each one write in the date when you expect to accomplish each item.

Groups

1. One of the important benefits members of the group can provide each other is support and accountability. Have individual members share their progress in developing the Budget Box, selecting a Track, purchasing the necessary items, or following through. (For instance, if they have decided to get an outside bookkeeper, what steps have they taken to arrange this?)

2. Suggestions for group leader: Keep a record of the commitments of each member, based on their input. Have each one indicate what items need to be completed to get "on track." Follow up in succeeding weeks to see how they are progressing, using compliments, praise and encouragement as motivators.

9

Looking Forward

Step 8: Plan five years in advance.

In the long run, men hit only what they aim at.
—Henry David Thoreau

The wise man looks ahead. The fool attempts to fool himself and won't face facts (Proverbs 14:8, TLB).

Janette was a gorgeous Phlegmatic who was married to Edward, a handsome Sanguine who was salesman of the year for his company. They had worked themselves out of the debt trap through persistence and willpower. But ten years later they still hadn't achieved the financial freedom they were seeking.

"Do you have a five-year plan?" I asked them.

"Yes, sort of," Edward replied.

"We have a general idea where we want to be financially in five years," Janette explained, "but it isn't exactly written down."

"Then let's make a written list of your goals," I suggested.

"We thought about doing that. But my job is subject to so many ups and downs. I work on commission and Janette is just finishing up her master's degree. We don't know how much money we'll be making over the next five years."

"That's right," Janette agreed. "How can we make a

long-term plan when the future is so uncertain?"

"You're never going to be living in a totally unchanging financial climate. But without a target you will never know if you have even come close to hitting the mark. A written five-year plan is a must to achieve the success you want."

Janette and Edward went home with a series of questions which would help them clarify their goals. A week later they had a written five-year plan.

The first benefit they noticed was an almost immediate sense of well-being. Having defined their aims, they felt they had achieved a significant step toward financial freedom. They found it much easier to stick to their budget knowing their objectives were clarified and achievable.

An Imperfect Plan Is Better Than None

I have yet to meet a financially troubled person who has a *detailed, realistic, written five-year plan.* There is something about putting goals in writing that represents a significant step forward. I don't know why this is so. Yet most of us resist this. It seems we like to daydream, but we hate to pin our dreams down to specifics.

Phlegmatics think a written plan is too much trouble. Sanguines can't make up their minds. Cholerics think they can carry their plans in their heads. And Melancholies don't want to make a plan until it is perfect.

Even if we start out with an imperfect plan at first, it can be changed, updated and improved.

When we write down our goals and the steps necessary to achieve them, we have put ourselves on the spot, so to speak. We are calling our own bluff. As soon as a goal is specific and we can see what it will take to achieve that goal, we don't have any more excuses.

And that's what it takes to succeed at finances or anything else. Stop giving yourself permission to fail. Pin yourself down to specifics with Step 8:

Step 8:
Plan five years in advance.

Six Strategies for Attaining Your Financial Objectives

1. Decide on your primary goals.

Almost any plan is better than no plan, because as soon as you start writing you will discover how fuzzy your thinking has been. You will be able to spot areas where you need to do more planning to arrive at a logical and achievable program.

2. Picture the rewards you will experience when you accomplish your primary goals.

All of us work harder when we let ourselves savor the rewards we will enjoy upon arriving at our destination. What will be your reward for paying off all your bills? A feeling of self-respect? No more telephone calls from angry creditors? An end to bitter arguments with your spouse over money matters? Give your imagination time to enjoy in advance the rewards of your efforts.

3. Plot out the intermediate steps necessary to achieve your primary goals.

Even seemingly awesome achievements become manageable when we break them up into small tasks. If you want to run a marathon, you don't begin your first day of training by thinking how fatiguing it will be to run 26.2 miles. You start out walking, jogging or running a small segment of the marathon distance—perhaps just half a mile. Each day you add a little more to your distance, even if it is just a few blocks. Eventually you will find, as I did, that you can indeed run, walk or jog a marathon.

4. Assign a deadline for each primary goal and each intermediate step.

Procrastination is the handmaiden of defeat. Set a deadline for achieving your main objective, then give yourself specific dates to accomplish each of the smaller steps which will take you there. This is like sending a message to your brain, "This is not a daydream. This is not a dress rehearsal. This is the real thing, and I mean business this time."

5. Work on the most important primary goal first.

List your primary goals in the order of their importance. Start work on the most important one first. When you have accomplished one goal, move on to the next. Don't try to change your whole financial future all at once. Be patient with yourself, but keep moving.

6. Pat yourself on the back often.

Those of us who have experienced financial failure tend to minimize our achievements and dwell on our failures. But psychologists tell us that the best way to change behavior in others is to praise them for every positive achievement. The same is true of changing your own performance. Praise yourself for sticking to your roadmap. Reward yourself with non-monetary prizes when you pass significant milestones along the way.

How to Build Your Five-Year Plan

Define Your Primary Goals

On the next page is a box that will help you define your primary goals. Place a check mark beside each of the items that is of concern to you. In the blank spaces provided, list other goals that are important.

WHAT ARE YOUR PRIMARY GOALS?

In the spaces below, place a check mark in the boxes next to the goals that you believe are your primary goals. On the empty lines, write in other primary goals. (These may be goals that will require more than five years to complete.)

		Target Date
☐	Get out of debt.	________
☐	Save ____ months' income.	________
☐	Start savings plan for auto.	________
☐	Start savings plan for home.	________
☐	Save down payment for home.	________
☐	______________________________	________
☐	______________________________	________
☐	______________________________	________
☐	______________________________	________
☐	______________________________	________
☐	______________________________	________

Now place a number beside each primary goal to rank them in order of personal importance to you. Transfer these goals to the box on the next page, SUMMARY OF PRIMARY GOALS.

Five-Year Plan:
SUMMARY OF PRIMARY GOALS

List below your primary goals, in the order of their importance.

PRIMARY GOALS	DEADLINE
1.______	______
2.______	______
3.______	______
4.______	______
5.______	______
6.______	______
7.______	______
8.______	______
9.______	______
10.______	______
11.______	______
12.______	______
13.______	______
14.______	______
15.______	______
16.______	______
17.______	______
18.______	______
19.______	______
20.______	______

Your Summary of Primary Goals might look something like this:

1. Tithe regularly.
2. Get out of debt.
3. Set aside three to six months' salary in savings.
4. Get life insurance for husband sufficient to support the family without wife's having to work until children are junior high school age.
5. Decrease spending 10 percent.
6. Increase income 10 percent.
7. Start long-term savings plan of 10 percent of net income.
8. Establish auto savings fund to purchase next car for cash.

Look back over the list. Notice that your goal 2, "Get out of debt," is dependent upon fulfilling goals 5 and 6.

"Decrease spending by 10 percent" and "Increase income by 10 percent" are intermediate steps that you would take to accomplish primary goal 2, "Get out of debt."

So the next step is to take each one of your primary goals and plan intermediate steps you will need to take to reach that primary goal.

On the following page is a sample primary goal planner. Use this form as a guide to make your own form or, if you prefer, make some photocopies of this form. Fill out one sheet for each primary goal, indicating the steps needed to achieve it and the rewards that will be experienced when the objective is reached.

Five-Year Plan:
PRIMARY GOAL PLANNER

Primary Goal (complete and vivid description):

Deadline date:

Rewards for Achieving Primary Goal:

Intermediate Steps to Achieving Primary Goal

Describe each intermediate step necessary to achieve this primary goal and determine a deadline.

Step	Deadline

The completed forms might look like this:

Five-Year Plan:
SUMMARY OF PRIMARY GOALS

List below your primary goals, in the order of their importance.

PRIMARY GOALS	DEADLINE
1. Increase giving to 10 percent	8/1/93
2. Three months' salary—savings	1/1/94
3. Pay cash for next car	11/1/96
4. Save $10,000 for college—Jenny	1998
5. Save $10,000 for college—Steve	2001
6.____________	______
7.____________	______
8.____________	______
9.____________	______
10.____________	______
11.____________	______
12.____________	______
13.____________	______
14.____________	______
15.____________	______
16.____________	______

Note: #4 and #5 will not be completed within five years, but will be *begun* within five years.

Five-Year Plan:
PRIMARY GOAL PLANNER

Primary Goal (complete and vivid description):

Save three months' salary ($2,500) to be held in interest-bearing account at Valley Bank

Deadline date: forty-eight months from now, 1/1/94

Rewards for Achieving Primary Goal:

peace of mind

sleep better, worry less

feelings of security and pride in accomplishment

ability to weather layoff, illness or job change

Intermediate Steps to Achieving Primary Goal

Describe each intermediate step necessary to achieve this primary goal and determine a deadline.

Step	Deadline
1. Open separate savings account	next Fri.
2. Arrange automatic deduction	next Fri.
3. Start deduction at $50 per paycheck	2 weeks
4. Increase deduction to $75	12 months

All of these are solid goals. They are sound, and they are placed in a reasonable order of priority; that is, they flow in a common-sense manner from the most pressing and realizable short-term goals to the most distant but still very achievable goals.

Your goals may be different. You may want to open your own business in five years. You may wish to decrease your spending so you can go back to college to earn a degree. However, I am going to recommend a basic list of primary goals that will ensure financial freedom. The primary goals should be these, and in more or less this order:

1. Get out of debt, or reduce it to no more than 20 percent of annual take-home pay.

2. Accumulate the equivalent of three to six months' wages in savings (wage security).

3. Have an ongoing bank account so that when your present car(s) need to be replaced, you can pay cash (auto security).

4. Have an ongoing savings account so you can pay for necessary home repairs, appliance replacements, etc., with cash (home security).

The above goals are basic—the rock-bottom security everyone should aim for. Beyond these, use your own and spouse's concerns, your network with opposites on your financial team, and your common sense to guide you.

Renew Your Five-Year Plan Every Year

Your five-year plan should be revised and updated at the end of every twelve-month period. The five-year plan does not run from January to January because I do not want you to wait until the new year starts to launch yourself on this program. Your five-year plan starts today, right now, whenever you decide to start it.

Your five-year plan includes primary goals and intermediate steps that will be accomplished in one, two, three or four years (or fractions of a year, such as eighteen months). The purpose of the five-year plan is to help you envision the long-range effects of your decisions and planning. You should revise and update it every year, copying to a new five-year plan those items that still remain to be accomplished. In other words, every year you will still be planning five years ahead.

When you review your five-year plan at the end of each twelve-month period, you will have a complete view of your accomplishments for the past year. You will see ways to improve. Best of all, you can praise yourself for the progress you have made.

Keep Your Goals Visible

Most of us get excited about a new program but within a few weeks we get side-tracked. Before long, the resolutions we made with such enthusiasm start to sprout green fuzz like last Monday's leftovers.

How can you keep your good intentions from going stale?

Some people find it helps to tell others about their decisions. Relatives can sometimes help us more than our friends, who may have a tendency to accept us just as we are, without regard for what we want to become. A client writes:

> I knew when we started on your financial program we were bucking years of bad habits. We have a tendency to get excited about something and then within a few weeks, we're back to our old ways. Like the gym we joined when we were determined to lose weight, and some of the diets we've tried. But we knew

one thing would keep us true to our Money Makeover—our pride. We knew if we told my in-laws about our new financial goals, that would help us stick to the program. In the past they have not been too kind in their remarks about our spending habits. We knew they were right, but that still made it hard to listen to their snide comments. Anyway, we knew that if we told Bill's parents about this new spending program, they would keep bringing it up . . . and if we went back to our old ways, we'd never hear the end of it. That turned out to be the wisest decision we could have made. We've stuck with our goals. We're now completely out of debt—which I just can't believe! We're saving for a down payment on a house. Bill's folks treat us differently, and the truth is, we feel different about ourselves.

My husband and I keep a small bulletin board in our bathroom where we see it every morning. I paid $5 for it at a hardware store and antiqued it a pale blue to match the wallpaper. On it we have posted our five-year plan. There is no way to forget the promises we have made to ourselves because they confront us every time we brush our teeth.

Don and Trina: Their Five-Year Plan

Remember Don and Trina from chapter 7? You walked with them step-by-step through their budget process and their decision to try to become totally debt-free in twenty-eight months. Their primary goals list of their five-year plan looked like this:

1. Get free of debt in twenty-eight months.

2. Save four months' wages (wage security) starting in twenty-eight months, to be accomplished in thirty-eight months.

3. Set aside money for vacation, starting in forty months (permanent and ongoing).

4. Set aside money for car (auto security) starting in twenty-eight months (permanent and ongoing).

5. Save for down payment on house starting in twenty-eight months—goal to be accomplished in sixty months.

By paying off their bills in twenty-eight months, they would free up hundreds of dollars they had formerly been paying in car and installment debt payments. Don received a raise at the end of the first year, which gave them $163 more per month. They increased clothing to $80 and allocated $100 per month in their budget for a permanent vacation fund. They started a permanent Auto Security fund which would permit them to pay cash for an $8,000 auto in forty-five months (twenty-eight months after starting their program, meaning that their present car would by that time be ten years old).

At the end of the twenty-eight months they were debt-free. That left $740 per month to save for two primary goals in their five-year plan: Accumulating four months' wages in a reserve savings account which would remain in place, and starting to save for a down payment on a house. By saving $740 per month, it took them seventeen months to accumulate four months' wages (approximately $12,000).

Only four-and-a-half years later they had achieved the following: paid all of their debts in full; accumulated $12,000 for wage security; saved enough for a yearly family vacation which will be a permanent part of their budget allocation every year; saved $2,600 toward their goal of paying cash for their next car. And they still had six months to go on their five-year plan.

After four-and-a-half years, their oldest child was in second grade and their youngest was enrolled in kindergarten. At that point, with the two children both in school, Trina decided to return to teaching school on a substitute basis. Her additional income contributed an average of $500 per month after taxes to the family income.

So, beginning only forty-eight months from the date they began their five-year plan, they were able to start saving approximately $1,000 a month. By the end of sixty months—the completion of their five-year plan—they had accumulated $8,736—more than half what they would need for a down payment on a home.

Based upon their gross earnings of $50,000, they figured they could afford a mortgage of $125,000. In order to buy a home with a value of $140,000 they wanted to be able to start with a down payment of $15,000. They achieved their largest goal of saving a down payment on a home just sixty-seven months from the time when they first began their first five-year plan.

How To Keep Your Goals Alive and Well

1. Keep them visible. Get a bulletin board or post them in a prominent place.
2. Tell a friend or relative who will remind you if you start to fail.
3. Remind yourself of your goals several times a day.
4. Memorize affirmations or scriptures to support your enthusiasm and repeat them to yourself several times each day.
5. Pat yourself on the back every time you take even one small step toward achieving your objectives.

Potholes on the Road to Financial Freedom

It is amazing how much we humans have in common with moles and ostriches. We like to keep ourselves in the dark. Take car repairs, for instance. I used to act as though my car were immortal. I never planned for repairs or maintenance, and always felt slightly betrayed when the poor old thing periodically collapsed. Fortunately I now have a husband who loves to tend to such things. (Remember *networking!*)

In the same way, I know many couples who have growing children but who haven't the slightest idea how (or if) they will pay for such things as college or weddings. I don't know why we avoid making plans for contingencies that are almost certain to occur. Perhaps it is because these events can be so expensive that we can't possibly imagine where we will find the money.

It is no use to worry about what we can't change. But often we avoid taking constructive action, over-estimating the challenge and thereby forfeiting the opportunity to take effective small actions that would greatly alleviate future problems.

Should You Be Making Financial Plans for These Milestones?

Weddings

Many people take for granted that their children will eventually marry, but make no financial provision whatever for the cost of weddings. We hear a lot these days about "saving for the kids' college." But I rarely hear anyone speak of having a savings account for weddings. Weddings generally cost thousands of dollars and generally it is the daughter's family who will foot the bill.

You may decide that your children should pay for their own weddings. You may hope they elope or that they will somehow get the idea on their own to start a savings account. Whatever the choice, a decision should be made and it should be made years in advance, if possible. After the decision is made, *communicate it to the children.* Many parents who do not plan in advance find themselves embroiled in bitter quarrels with their children over such things as photographers, dresses and flowers when they should be treasuring their last precious weeks together as a family.

College

If you plan to assist your children with college, don't wait until they are in high school to start a college fund. Decisions like these should be made as early as possible—preferably, even before you begin to have children.

Don and Trina were determined to avoid the problem that their parents had encountered. While Don was growing up his parents spent all their available money on enjoyable things like camping trips, vacations and toys. Don remembers having a fun-filled childhood. But he feels short-changed that his parents did not plan financially for his college—something that would affect him his entire life.

Don and Trina felt strongly that they wanted to encourage their children to attend college, but paying for four years at a private institution was beyond their means. They decided to set up a college fund which would provide $10,000 for each child by the time each reached their senior year in high school.

They knew that this would not pay the full costs of their children's educations. However, this is all they could afford. Beyond that amount, they felt that each child would have to be responsible to finance his or her own education, either by part-time work, student loans or scholarships.

What if there simply does not seem to be any money available for a college fund?

Bob and Jan have six children in their blended family. Although Bob is a dentist working for a group practice, theirs is a second marriage and income barely covers expenses. Here is how Bob is planning for his children's college:

> I worked my way through college and dental school, holding down a full-time job. We are doing all we can just to pay our regular bills, give to our church, and keep a roof over our heads.
>
> Our kids are talented, but none of them has achieved sufficient scholastic standing to ensure that they will be granted scholarships based on their grades. In our salary bracket, we make too much for them to be entitled to student aid. The only other alternative is student loans and part-time jobs.
>
> There are many good schools and colleges close by, including several state colleges within thirty minutes' driving distance. Our contribution to their college education will be to see that they get room and board, as well as encouragement, for as long as they want to attend school—through graduate school, whatever.

Many people get bogged down in despair because they don't see how a small savings program can make a significant difference to their children's futures. They look at the soaring costs of a college education and figuratively throw up their hands. Or they put off making a decision to start a college fund, in the belief that they will be better able to afford it at some time in the future.

Whatever the ages of your children, now is a good time to examine all the alternatives, discuss them with your children and work as a family toward achieving a realistic educational plan that is within your means.

Private School

Don and Trina began their five-year plan with serious questions about future schooling for their children. When they started their plan, the children were ages three years and eighteen months, respectively. Their preference was to send their children to private schools. When they examined their financial situation, however, they realized they could not afford the tuition.

One Sunday, in chatting about their concerns with a group of young parents at church, Trina learned that there was a national network of parents providing support and information on home schooling, and that in 1988 there were 3,000 home school permits issued in California. She learned that she could join with other home-schooling parents for field trips, problem-solving, recreation and other enrichment programs.

They met with other parents who were active in home schooling to find out what was involved. Trina found she could home-teach and still work part-time through a cooperative effort with other home-schooling parents.

Although this eventually turned out to be the perfect answer for Don and Trina, home schooling is not for everyone. It takes a major commitment of time, energy and patience. But if you cannot afford private schooling, home school might be the right decision for you.

How to Rebuild Damaged Credit

As some point every one of my clients will ask me, "What can I do to repair my credit?" Throughout this book I have stressed the dangers of unrestrained use of credit, but there are a few situations in which you may want to use credit.

Most people cannot afford to pay cash for a home. Since real estate generally appreciates, and there are tax advantages to owning a home, it is wise to plan for the purchase of a home as long as it is in within your income.

Automobiles are large purchases and frequently must be financed, even though it is preferable to pay cash. I advise my clients to save and pay cash for their automobiles, buying one that is at least one year old with low mileage. This one discipline could save you enough in interest over the next twenty years to put your children through college.

A third use for credit may be student loans to further your own education or that of your children.

If misfortune or bad spending decisions have gotten you in trouble with your creditors, here are some basic steps you can take to rebuild your financial credibility.

1. *Open a savings account at a local bank.* Make it a point to introduce yourself to the manager or other bank official. Explain that you have had financial problems in the past and that you are now earnestly attempting to rebuild your credit reputation and your financial stability. State that you are there to open an account at the bank, and that the purpose of introducing yourself personally is that you would like to call upon the bank's services from time to time for financial advice.

2. *Save regularly and in person.* Do not use the automatic teller machine to make your deposits. Do not mail them to the bank. Each week, go into the bank with your deposit. Smile at the teller, say hello to the bank manager you met on your first visit. Remember the names of bank personnel and be sure to greet them. And smile. A smile costs nothing but earns interest and pays dividends.

3. *After you have been saving for a year or more and have accumulated $1,000 or more in your savings account, apply for a loan.* By the time you have gone into the bank fifty-two times or more, you will be known by name and you will have made a more favorable impression.

(a) Approach the bank officer or manager whom you met on your first visit, or one of the other employees who now knows your name and is aware of your frequent trips to the bank.

(b) Ask for a loan of $1,000. Tell the loan officer that you would like to pledge as security $1,000 of savings that you already have in the bank so that the bank is not going to be taking a risk on you (Loan #1).

4. *Open a second savings account at Bank #2.* Deposit in that savings account the proceeds of Loan #1.

5. *Pay off Loan #1 over a period of one year.* Make your monthly payments on time without fail. At the end of the second year, you will have two savings accounts with two different banks, and a favorable loan record with Bank #1.

6. *Apply for a secured loan (Loan #2) at Bank #2,* duplicating the process covered in Step #3b above.

7. *Open a savings account at Bank #3.* Deposit the proceeds of Loan #2 at a new savings account to be opened up at Bank #3.

By the time you have completed this process you will have a good credit record at two banks, with loans faithfully paid on time. You will have savings accounts at three banks. You will have established a personal relationship with personnel at each of these three banks. You will no longer be merely an anonymous account number. You will be a friend and a loyal, dependable customer.

Most important, you will have taken giant steps toward rebuilding your credit rating and your self-respect.

Savings: Think Big and Start Small

In the office of a friend of mine there is a brass-plated plaque that proclaims the message: *THINK BIG—but start small.*

As a banker involved in lending to small businesses, he has found that this philosophy is only halfway acceptable to most Americans. Most of us like to think big—but we don't want to start small. "In this country we have been told so often to think big, we don't appreciate the value of the small details of living," he told me.

Nowhere is this more apparent than in the area of savings. Think about the small ways you can cut back spending. Think about setting aside nickels, dimes and quarters, in addition to dollars. Even small amounts, saved over a long period, can turn your life around.

If you set aside $3.28 a day, you will be saving $100 a month. If you continue this practice and put the savings in an account earning 8 percent interest, in three years you will have $4,053. In five years you will have $7,347.

In ten years you will have $18,294.

In twenty years you will have $58,902!

Most of us are impatient. We fantasize about quick solutions. But fast fixes are usually the stuff of daydreams, not reality.

You can solve your financial problems, working methodically, one step at a time, one day at a time.

Think big. Plan to reach your highest goals. At the same time, don't be discouraged if you must "start small." The important thing is to start. Start with assurance. And start now.

$ $ $

Suggestions for Personal and Group Study

Individuals

1. If you have made out your five-year plan, you should congratulate yourself. You are in an elite class! Did you know that less than 3 percent of all people actually have a written plan for their future?

2. Take a moment to review the progress you have made. Have you experienced a change of attitude about debt? Are you experiencing more order and control? How does it feel to know what your goals are and have a plan for accomplishing them?

3. Review your decision lists and savor once again the rewards you will experience once you have reached your goal.

4. Place your list of primary goals in a place where you will see them every day.

Groups

Have the members bring their five-year plans to the meeting and compare and discuss them, asking the following questions:

1. How far did they get in completing the plans? (Congratulate them for what they accomplished, reminding them that even a partial plan is a start—and cause for encouragement.)

2. Did they run into problems in any areas? Discuss these, and form teams or smaller groups to help those who have run into difficulties and want assistance.

10

When You Feel All Hope Is Lost

Step 9: Consider bankruptcy only as a last resort.

At the end of every seven years you must cancel debts. This is how it is to be done: Every creditor shall cancel the loan he has made to his fellow Israelite. He shall not require payment from his fellow Israelite or brother, because the Lord's time for canceling debts has been proclaimed (Deuteronomy 15:1,2, NIV).

Wilt thou seal up the avenues of ill?
Pay every debt, as if God wrote the bill.
—Ralph Waldo Emerson

"My situation is beyond the reach of credit counselors, Debtors Anonymous or any other relief I can think of. I'm at the end of my rope!"

Is this the way you feel, even after spending time going through all of the steps in the Money Makeover? Are you in a predicament where you need drastic intervention, such as

- Foreclosure on your home
- Back taxes due
- Unmanageable, unpayable debts
- A business in trouble
- A lawsuit that could cost you almost everything

As we will see in this chapter, there are several different types of legal relief that are available, depending upon the nature of your problem.

What we're talking about is the B word: *bankruptcy*. Now I know that this is a dirty word to many people—especially those who consider it a moral responsibility (as I do) to pay one's debts. Bankruptcy is indeed a traumatic experience which has lasting side-effects, the least of which are damage to one's reputation and self-esteem. Yet, for the unfortunate few whose only alternative might be homelessness and destitution, bankruptcy laws can provide some legal protection.

Unfortunately, there are some people in every society who will misuse, or take advantage of, the precious liberties we have. Our bankruptcy laws were certainly not designed to provide a convenient way to avoid the ethical and legal responsibilities of just debt. Later in this chapter we'll discuss some of the ways that bankruptcy should *not* be used.

The decision to file bankruptcy is a personal and highly individual one which should be undertaken only after the most careful consideration. Bankruptcy's memory will linger for ten years on your credit report. It is an extreme measure and should be absolutely the last solution you should consider. But if you feel all other hope is lost, it may be time to

Step 9:
Consider bankruptcy only as a last resort.

How to decide? Following are some case studies of people who considered bankruptcy.

Illness

They were a couple in their early sixties, well-dressed and dignified. Harry and Dora wore the shattered look of people who were facing the greatest humiliation of their lives. They could not pay their bills.

I asked them for a list of their assets and learned that despite a lifetime of hard work, they did not own a home—an unusual circumstance for people of their generation.

"We sold our home to pay medical bills," they told me.

"What is the fair market value of your furniture?" I probed.

"We sold everything to buy food."

"Where are you living now?"

"Some friends of ours have a trailer out in the country near Palm Desert. They told us we could live there without paying rent."

How had they gotten into such a mess? Harry had been doing well in his job as a salesman until he had a heart attack at the age of fifty-six. After a three-month leave of absence he was told by his doctors that he was well enough to return to work. But within a couple of months, Harry was laid off. The illness had slowed him down—he was having problems with his short-term memory and he could not keep up his sales quota.

Harry's health insurance was provided by his employer, so it was cancelled when he was laid off. He was able to convert to a private policy for a few months. When he contacted other insurance companies he was told that there would be an exclusion for his pre-existing condition. The stress of trying to find new employment brought on additional physical problems. When he went to the doctor for a follow-up examination, he was told that he would have to undergo bypass surgery.

The bypass was a success, but the financial results were disastrous. By this time, Harry and Dora's savings were exhausted. Even after selling their home, they still had $35,000 in unpaid medical bills. That's when Harry and Dora started selling their furniture to buy food and moved to their friends' mobile home in the desert.

By then they were completely destitute. They were living on Harry's state disability and Dora's earnings from a part-time job as a waitress in a Palm Desert cafe. They could not afford to make even token payments on their bills. The threatening phone calls came steadily, sometimes late at night, from collectors who told them, "We must have $100 a month on this debt or we will sue you." (Even though late-night phone calls by collection agents have been declared illegal, they are by no means a rarity.)

I advised against their filing bankruptcy because they had so few assets, and all of them were exempt from action by creditors.

"We just can't take the stress of these creditor phone calls any longer," Dora said as she handed me a summons. "Now we're being sued. All our lives we've paid our bills on time. We've never collected welfare or unemployment. Now that we need help we're being treated like criminals. We've done all we can; all we want is some peace."

Business Failure

Peter looked every inch the successful executive: custom-tailored suit, handsome wrist watch, fine Italian shoes. The only clue to his inner turmoil were the dark shadows under his eyes.

He shook his head slowly and hunched over in his chair, staring at the floor. "I can't believe this is happening," he muttered over and over. "For the past seventeen years I've owned a successful men's clothing store. I just can't believe I'm facing bankruptcy."

What had happened to a lifetime of success? First Peter was caught in a business cycle of rapidly escalating overhead costs and narrowing profit margins. Construction on a nearby interstate freeway isolated his store from the flow of customer traffic. Then a manager quit, leaving the books in a mess.

As sales slumped, Peter struggled to keep afloat by taking out short-term loans at the market rate, which at that time was 18 percent. The business loans were secured by deeds of trust on his home. He figured business would pick up over the holidays. But business did not pick up, and now the creditors were threatening to close him down.

I confirmed what he already knew. In a Chapter 7 bankruptcy he would lose his home, everything. At fifty years of age, Peter was down and out. Even though he did not seem to be the sort of man to break under pressure, his eyes became moist with bitter tears as he spoke.

"We're going to lose our home, our savings are wiped out, and I don't have a job. I've been looking for work, but there isn't much out there for guys my age."

"Let's look at the possibility of a business reorganization," I said.

He seemed not to hear me. "My wife's upset because we're losing the house. Even my kids are mad at me. My son was planning to start Stanford this fall. I told him there's no way I can swing the tuition—he'll have to go to a state college."

Then Peter said something which I hear all too frequently but which always makes me glad I can offer not only legal help but the love of the Great Comforter. Nevertheless, the words bring a chill each time I hear them.

"I still have my life insurance," he said. "I'd probably do everybody a favor if I could just get up the nerve to commit suicide."

Lawsuits

Maureen was a single mother, the sole support of two children, who owned a small home from which she operated a graphic design business. She was making ends meet until one of her major customers started having his own financial problems and began to be late paying his bills. He owed Maureen $5,600 which did not seem like a large amount to the customer, but to Maureen it amounted to almost three months' income.

As the customer fell further and further behind in his account, Maureen started getting behind on her own payments. When her auto insurance premium became due she had a choice: Pay the insurance or buy groceries. She bought food; the insurance policy lapsed. Before she could get the money together to reinstate her insurance, Maureen was involved in an automobile accident in which a passenger in the other car was badly injured.

Even though Maureen felt the accident was not her fault, the other party filed suit. Maureen was served with court papers telling her she had thirty days to file a response. She tried to find a lawyer to represent her but found that she would have to spend several thousand dollars in fees to go to trial to defend her position. With no money to hire a lawyer, the thirty days ran out. The plaintiff obtained a default judgment against her in the amount of $50,000, and recorded a judgment lien on her home. Maureen was now faced with the loss of her home because the judgment gave the plaintiff the right to sell her home to recover his money.

If she sold her home to pay part of the judgment, she

would be forced to live in an apartment. Even a two-bedroom apartment in an undesirable neighborhood would cost $200 more than her current house payment. Maureen was worried about the effects of moving her children into an unsafe neighborhood, let alone how she was going to increase her business to make up for her lost income stream.

Unwise Use of Credit

When the unsolicited credit cards started arriving in the mail, Dan had no intention of becoming a credit junkie. He was just pleased with the tangible evidence that he had "arrived," and thought he would use the cards only for emergencies.

He had just graduated from college, landed his first job as an aerospace engineer, and leased a bachelor apartment near work. After treating himself to a new compact car, he started buying a few items of furniture on credit. He was sure he would be able to make all the payments. No problem.

Then Dan met Bobbi and fell in love. Suddenly his expenses took a sharp upward turn. There were romantic dinners, flowers and gifts. There were leisurely Sunday brunches and long drives up the coast. The credit cards helped disguise the high cost of loving. Within two months they were married in a large, splashy ceremony that further expanded Dan's ballooning loan balances.

In order to increase his take-home pay, Dan increased the number of his tax exemptions. The result was that, when he filed his tax return, he owed a substantial tax bill. Dan panicked. His taxes were accruing penalties and interest faster than he could pay them. The revenue agent informed him that if he didn't make his peace soon with the IRS, they would start garnishing his wages. Dan knew that if his employer found out he had been so irresponsible, his job would be in serious jeopardy.

Dan's bubble of false prosperity based on deficit spending burst. As the dawn of reality spread its light into his financial affairs, his marriage began to falter. They began to have nasty arguments about money and other matters. After one particularly heated discussion, Bobbi walked out of his life.

Dan was crazy with despair. His whole world had crumbled around him. He was twenty-three years old and life had lost its meaning.

By the time Dan got over his initial heartsickness he realized he was hopelessly in debt. His bills equalled more than 1.5 times his annual take-home pay. With interest accruing at an average rate of 18 percent on his credit cards, it would take him 138 months—more than eleven years—to pay off all his bills at the rate of $500 per month. The IRS was breathing down his neck, and he feared loss of his job because of failure to meet his tax obligations.

Fortunately, Bobbi had not completely given up on him. Together they began seeing a counselor to discuss possible reconciliation. Then Bobbi gave him an ultimatum: Either get his finances under control or the romance was permanently off.

A Family Farm Faces Extinction

For three generations the Koch family operated a 200-acre plot of ground where they subsisted during hard times by occasionally taking a second job in town. Even though Mike kept expenses to a minimum, after three years of bad weather and crop failures he was unable to make the payments on his bank loans. Foreclosure loomed. Then, just when Mike's crops were coming in, the equipment leasing company told him they were going to repossess their harvester. In addition, there were back taxes to be paid.

Mike saw his way of life vanishing. Even though life on the farm was not easy, it was the way he had been raised—and he loved the land. He didn't want to give up; he hoped to pass the land on to his son. If only he could stretch his payments out for a few years, he was sure he could bring in a good harvest and make a go of his operation.

Loss of Income

Al and Geneva didn't believe in credit cards. They paid cash for everything and if they couldn't afford something they did without. By carefully shepherding their earnings, after seven years they were able to put a down payment on a house. Al liked his job, and they were active in the young marrieds group at church.

Due to appreciation of real estate and improvements they had made themselves, their house was increasing in value. Al was looking forward to a promotion in the fall. Their happiness was complete when Geneva became pregnant. The future looked rosy.

One day, without warning, all their hopes were shattered. Al went on a camping trip with the church youth group and, during a hike, fell and fractured two vertebrae. He required surgery and was out of work for seven months. Disability payments did not cover all of their expenses. They fell six months behind in their house payments. In addition, they had a car payment and bills totalling $4,800. Doctors were threatening to sue over unpaid medical bills.

When they came to see me, their house was set for foreclosure sale in two weeks. Their house was valued at $145,000 with encumbrances totalling $80,000. That meant they would lose $65,000 of equity in their home unless something could be done to stop the foreclosure.

Legal Protection Is Available

Each of these stories is an example of the thousands of people who are struggling, sometimes through no fault of their own, with mountains of debt.

Is there a way for Al and Geneva to save their home from foreclosure and pay their bills?

Is there a way for Maureen to avoid the judgment on her home which will otherwise force her to lose it and move to an unsafe neighborhood with her two children?

Is there a way for Harry and Dora to stop creditors from harassing them?

Can Mike stop the IRS and the leasing company and the bank from taking over his farm?

Can Peter hold off his creditors long enough to try to salvage what is left of his business?

And as for Dan and Bobbi—foolish couple—is there a way for them to pay their creditors, including the IRS, and prevent wage garnishment?

Yes!

There is relief under the Bankruptcy Code for every one of these situations.

Al and Geneva can stop the foreclosure and take up to three years to catch up their back house payments by filing a Chapter 13 bankruptcy.

Maureen can file a Chapter 7 bankruptcy and a subsequent motion to avoid the judgment lien on her home, eliminating the $50,000 judgment which she could not afford to fight in court.

Dan and Bobbi can file a Chapter 13 which will let them pay their credit card debt, and even their back taxes, taking up to five years to pay without incurring further interest or penalties.

Mike can file a Chapter 12 and save his farm, take

six years to pay his back taxes, and restructure his loans and equipment lease.

Peter can file a Chapter 11 business reorganization, which will give him time to find refinancing, move to a better location or sell his business assets at the highest possible price—a resolution that will yield more to his creditors than simply going out of business. He has time to decide what is best for his business, his employees and his creditors. He can continue to operate his business while he finds the best solution.

The Negatives of Bankruptcy

Does all this sound almost too good to be true? Don't be misled. Even though bankruptcy has many benefits, it also carries with it a number of negative aspects.

First and most obvious is that the record of bankruptcy will remain with your credit report for ten years. After filing bankruptcy it is difficult to get credit, perhaps for years. Personally, I do not view this as the most important negative result of bankruptcy. I am always dismayed when people, having just filed bankruptcy, agonize about how they can get back into the debt trap. It reminds me of the words in Proverbs 26:11: "Like a dog that returns to his vomit is a fool that repeats his folly" (RSV).

The loss of credit is not as devastating as the impact on your reputation and your self-respect. Once having filed, the act cannot be undone. It stays with you forever. Some types of employment are negatively impacted by bankruptcy. If you work in the banking industry, need a security clearance for your job, or if the job requires you to be bonded, you may find it difficult to find work or get job promotions.

Don't overlook the drawbacks. Bankruptcy is not a "free ride."

After Bankruptcy, What Next?

Even though the law relieves you of the obligation to repay your debts, I believe that morally we have duties that reach beyond our present bankruptcy statutes. I am speaking of repayment of debt, even though you may not be legally obligated to do so.

I know of one person who filed bankruptcy and who later won several million dollars in the state lottery. Despite the fact that he had the ability to repay all the debts listed on his bankruptcy, he did not do so.

Yet I know of another couple, Craig and Maria, who were forced by unforeseeable business circumstances to file both personal and business bankruptcy. In the years since that time, however, they have made every effort to pay off the debts that were discharged in the bankruptcy. Bit by bit, they are paying their debts, as they are enabled to do so.

Sometimes we confuse legality with morality. We get mixed up between what is "right" and what is "required." In a system of government based on law, many people tend to think that if the law *allows* something, it is *right.* But God is not so ready to let us off the hook. If, after filing bankruptcy, you find that you have the ability to pay your debts, consider the moral option. I encourage you to go beyond the law to do what is right as well as what is legal. Your reputation and your self-esteem will improve, and so will your walk with God.

Definitions of Different Types of Bankruptcy

Chapter 7

Chapter 7 bankruptcy is a so-called "straight" bankruptcy, which wipes out most unsecured debts such as credit cards, personal loans and charge accounts. Consensual loans on real estate, such as deeds of trust or mortgages, are not wiped out in a bankruptcy. Neither are liens which come about when you take out a loan wherein you pledge your household goods as collateral, or when you buy things on time, such as an automobile or furniture.

Non-possessory, non-purchase-money liens on household goods (those contracts where you borrow money and pledge as collateral those things you already own) can be avoided in a bankruptcy by the filing of a separate motion in conjunction with the bankruptcy process. Judgment liens survive bankruptcy but they may also be avoided to the extent that they impair exemptions on property.

Some examples of the types of debts which are not dischargeable are: student loans, taxes less than three years old, alimony and child support, and debts which result from the debtor's driving under the influence of alcohol.

Chapter 11

When a partnership, corporation or individual needs time to restructure, reorganize or refinance an ailing enterprise, Chapter 11 can provide an avenue of relief. Chapter 11 proceedings are complex in nature, require the services of a bankruptcy attorney, and are generally far more costly in terms of attorneys' fees, court costs and accountants' fees than Chapter 7.

In Chapter 11 a business may take several years to pay past debts, and may pay only a portion of such obligations as long as creditors receive at least as much as they would if the business were liquidated under Chapter 7. The debtor may pay back taxes, taking up to six years from the date of the assessment to do so, plus interest (but no penalties) at the current IRC (Internal Revenue Code) rate of interest.

Chapter 12

A petition under Chapter 12 is similar in many respects to the debt restructuring provisions available to wage-earners under Chapter 13 or corporations under Chapter 11. To be eligible for Chapter 12 protection, the debtor must be a family farmer with regular income. Debts, including taxes, may be extended over a longer period of time; certain types of contracts and leases may be revised or repudiated. As in Chapter 11, the debtor will file with the court a proposed plan of adjustment of debts which must provide creditors at least as much as they would receive were the family farm to be sold and all assets liquidated.

Chapter 13

Chapter 13 provides debt relief for individuals (not corporations) and can be used to pay back debts, stop foreclosures or wage garnishments, and pay back taxes. The Chapter 13 plan must represent the best efforts of the debtor, and provide creditors at least as much as they would receive in a Chapter 7 liquidation. Debtors may take three years, or up to five years in some instances, to repay their debts. In order to be eligible, debtors must have no more than $100,000 in unsecured debt, and no more than $350,000 in secured debt.

You can pay back taxes through a Chapter 13 plan, with no added interest or penalties after the date of filing of the petition.

Exemptions

Some people are afraid they will lose all of their belongings if they file bankruptcy, or that someone from the court will come into their home and begin to haul away their possessions.

It does not make economic sense to throw people out

into the street and strip them of every asset. Thus Congress enacted the Bankruptcy Code to give debtors a "fresh start." Congress made up a list of belongings which should receive special protection from creditors. The laws related to these items are called "exemption statutes."

In addition to the federal exemption statutes, each of the states has the right to enforce its own exemption standards. These differ markedly from one state to another. Some states provide their citizens very little in the way of a fresh start, i.e., they can keep very few of their possessions. Other states have very liberal exemption statutes.

Generally, you are entitled to keep a home or some equity in your home, tools of your trade, a transportation automobile, clothing and household furnishings.

You are entitled to all of the protections available to you by law without feeling guilty. This is not being selfish, greedy or dishonest. It is good stewardship to exercise prudent legal planning for the sake of yourself and your family.

When you are insolvent, you are entitled to certain legal protections, just as you are entitled to various tax breaks based upon changes in circumstances. For the person who seeks to live by the timeless standards of the Holy Bible, there is no biblical injunction against taking every available legal exemption. Your lawyer will insist that you do so; to fail to claim the available exemptions is legal malpractice and a breach of your attorney's duty which would call his/her reputation strongly into question.

The main purpose of exemptions is to ensure that you will not have to rely on public assistance or welfare but will be able to regain sufficient economic strength so you can resume paying sales tax, income tax, gasoline tax, and contributing once more to the economy. As a taxpayer, as a responsible member of society, you are entitled to the rehabilitative effects of exemptions and the dignity of the fresh start that Congress specifically enacted for you.

The Bible: A Financial Guide for All Time

The Old Testament is full of references to financial matters. It provides keen insights into God's thoughts concerning the way we are to spend, save and give. The Bible contains more references to finances than to heaven! God clearly established principles for generosity, caring for the poor and forgiveness of debt. The Israelites were even forbidden to charge interest on loans to their kinsmen.

What did God instruct Moses?

> At the end of every seven years you must cancel debts. This is how it is to be done: Every creditor shall cancel the loan he has made to his fellow Israelite. He shall not require payment from his fellow Israelite or brother, because the Lord's time for canceling debts has been proclaimed (Deuteronomy 15:1,2, NIV).

By the time Jesus walked the earth, the Jews had been practicing the tradition of debt forgiveness for thousands of years. It was an accepted part of their culture and economy. The New Testament records that Jesus accepted and supported this ancient practice which had been enunciated by God to Moses. In Matthew 18:21-35, Jesus speaks of an observance that was common to the time and within the experience of his listeners. That custom was forgiveness of debt.

The parable is to be understood on its spiritual and symbolic level. It was clearly understood by Jesus' listeners because it was a practice sanctioned by generations of the faithful. The higher meaning in Jesus' story cannot be separated from the simplicity of the message of forgiveness of debt.

God knows our natures. He knew that His people would make mistakes. They would not always follow divine wisdom in money matters or in any other area of life. At times they would be imprudent, make rash decisions. There also would be natural disasters and calamities which would overtake man in his fallen state. So in loving patience He made provision for our times of weakness and failure.

When Liberty Becomes License

Even though the laws of our nation, and the Bible, give us the liberty to make the decision on whether or not to file, no discussion of bankruptcy can be complete without a look at the obvious—and all-too-frequent—abuses which this system invites. I personally have seen many situations where bankruptcy was grossly misused. I have even known people who are comfortable labeling themselves as Christians who blithely walked away from debt, misapplying the scriptural references to debt forgiveness. The Bible also teaches that the just man pays his debts. "The wicked borrow and do not repay, but the righteous give generously" (Psalm 37:21, NIV). One of the worst areas of abuse is between family and friends.

Dean was twenty-three years old and starting a new job. His old car was virtually falling apart, but he did not have sufficient credit standing to be able to buy a car on his own. He asked his parents to become co-obligors with him on a security agreement which would enable him to purchase a car. They agreed, reasoning that their son needed transportation to get to and from work.

Within a few months, Dean began to miss payments. His parents started making the payments for him. They noticed, however, that Dean still managed to find money for other things which were important to him. He had money for restaurant meals with friends and for fun trips. After he had missed several payments, they asked him to turn over the car to them, but he refused. How would he get to work? he asked. They asked him to make at least partial payments, to the extent of his ability to do so, but he made vague excuses. Eventually, Dean's parents paid off the car in full, though they had to struggle financially to do so. They realized that if they did not make the payments, their own credit would be ruined. They did not want to repossess the car because they were afraid to ruin their relationship with their son. In fact, they were enabling him to continue in his pattern of irresponsibility.

Bart had a great idea for a business. He knew it would prosper because he planned to hire only Christians, and the project was, he believed, based on godly principles. He was sure God wanted him to be prosperous and be his own boss. With the divine blessing he was sure was his, he couldn't possibly fail. With confidence, he approached several couples at his church and asked them to invest in his business. Some of these members were new Christians and were very excited about their recently found faith. Bart convinced them that God was a co-partner in his new venture, and they readily agreed by signing over substantial sums of money to help him get started.

Within two years it became obvious that God's plans for Bart's business did not include economic success. The business failed, and the life savings of several couples disappeared with it. One couple had taken out a $20,000 second trust deed on their home in order to invest in Bart's venture. They are still making the payments, years later. Bart has shrugged this whole thing off as a "business deal" which failed. He is off on another business scheme, attending a new church, and talking about big bucks to those who will listen and pull out their checkbooks.

Hallie has always had a yen for the finer things of life. She likes silk blouses and designer jeans. She drives a late-model sports car. Every few years she gets in a financial bind because her paycheck doesn't match her tastes. When her creditors get fed up with her, she can usually find a boyfriend, a friend or a relative who will loan her the money to get caught up. She doesn't have a budget. And she has now had to file bankruptcy twice. But, she figures, so what? If things get tough, she'll move back home with her parents and let them support her awhile until she gets caught up on her bills. Or maybe she'll even marry somebody rich who will take care of her. If you criticize Hallie for her flagrant misuse of trust—both the trust of commercial creditors as well as of personal acquaintances—she'll tell you to mind your own business and not be so uptight. Fiscal responsibility is not high on her list of desired virtues.

I have known many people like this, both in my practice and in my personal life. So have you. Such behavior is irresponsible, dishonest and ungodly. By no stretch of the imagination could these kinds of actions be considered within the realm of biblical conduct. Although the Bible does not automatically condemn us for making financial mistakes, it does not give us a license to abuse others' trust. Whether the person you owe money to is a commercial lender you have never met, or a parent or friend, you cannot hide behind the Bible and use it as an authority for financial irresponsibility.

While the Bible is clear that we must forgive those who have injured us, nowhere does it require us to loan or give money to people who have previously proven to be untrustworthy as borrowers. Many times God has a lesson to teach people about trust and honesty in money dealings, but we get in the way of His lesson plan by providing them with a cushion or an easy way out. Financial irresponsibility is much like other forms of immaturity, addiction or compulsive behavior. You would not give liquor to an alcoholic, nor the money to purchase it.

One solution for dealing with financially irresponsible people is to simply stop loaning or giving them money, or the equivalent of money in any form. That includes letting them borrow your car or live under your roof. We have a responsibility to let people grow up, and that includes permitting them to enjoy the consequences of their foolish behavior.

Bankruptcy and the Constitution

Our modern bankruptcy laws evolved from the standards that God gave Moses. Early Americans came to these shores to escape not only religious bigotry and political persecution, but economic cruelty as well. Because our Founding Fathers felt strongly about the establishment of godly economics in the new nation, they included mention of bankruptcy laws in the earliest attempts at framing our laws.

The Constitution provides, at Article I, Section 8 that Congress should enact uniform laws concerning bankruptcy.

> The Congress shall have Power to lay and collect Taxes . . . to establish . . . uniform Laws on the subject of Bankruptcies throughout the United States.

Eventually debtors' prisons, indentured servitude and slavery were abolished as the country moved into the Industrial Era. Banks and businessmen began to extend credit to ranchers, prospectors and consumers. Debt kept the factories humming.

The business community began to thrive on the

credit system. Banks were making more money than ever before. Because it was believed to be beneficial to the national economy, laws were gradually enacted which would protect debtors who, for one reason or another, took on more debt than they could repay. Debting became the national pastime, for good—and for ill.

A Higher Standard

The administration of bankruptcy cases comes under the supervision of the United States Trustee, which is an arm of the Justice Department. What happens when someone deliberately falsifies documents or lies in a bankruptcy case? Or tries to hide assets, either by nondisclosure or by a pattern of fraudulent transfers prior to filing? Since our bankruptcy laws are a creature of federal statute, the Federal Bureau of Investigation is called in to investigate such cases.

The penalties for bankruptcy fraud are severe, involving imprisonment in a federal penitentiary and substantial fines. When an individual signs bankruptcy papers, he is required to sign an oath or affirmation that the information in the documents is true, correct and complete.

It is a serious crime to attempt to hide your assets. It is fraud to place assets in another person's name in an effort to conceal them from creditors. Any attempt to conceal property, including fraudulent transfers, could result in your bankruptcy discharge being disallowed or even criminal penalties.

Take advantage of every lawful protection which is available to you to enhance your prospects for getting a strong fresh start after bankruptcy. But do not for one moment toy with the idea of trying to conceal assets or defraud creditors, no matter how great the temptation or how much you may stand to lose.

God expressly forbids wanton disregard of our responsibilities. When we engage in a pattern of laziness, irresponsibility or foolishness, we are out of God's will. By the same token, it is not biblical to let people take advantage of us for their own selfish, whimsical or immature purposes. When we let ourselves be duped into assuming obligations which should not be ours to shoulder, we are not acting as wise stewards. We are simply promoting habits of poor stewardship in others.

But God makes a distinction between fraud and occasional frailty. Our present bankruptcy courts do also.

Our principal concern should be to conduct ourselves in a manner that will not bring discredit to our Lord. We should hold ourselves to a higher standard of conduct in all matters, and certainly this should apply in such a sensitive area as bankruptcy. This is a time to exercise faith and trust in God. He is watching with great interest to see what you will do during this time of testing.

And so are many others.

$ $ $

Suggestions for Personal and Group Study

Individuals

1. Have you in the past felt that you were out of God's will because of the way you were handling money?

2. Did your mismanagement of money create a feeling in you that there was a distance between you and God?

3. How did you respond to such feelings?

4. Have you found a better way of responding?

Groups

1. Why do you think God built into the Mosaic Code a provision for forgiveness of debt? Why did God take such an active and specific part in Israel's financial practices, such as the prohibition against charging interest on loans?

2. How do we react when someone owes us money and they do not pay us back? Anger? Resentment? Gossip or slander?

3. Do the circumstances of unpaid debt make a difference? Under what circumstances would we be better able to accept (forgive) a person's failure to pay a debt they owed us?

4. What should we do when another owes us money and fails to pay? Ignore him? Try to talk to him in love to find out what his circumstances are? Threaten legal action?

5. Even though we may say we believe that everything in the earth is the Lord's, including all money, why do we react as though the money were, in fact, ours and not God's when someone fails to repay a debt they owe us?

6. What has this lesson taught about the necessity for being prudent in the borrowing and the loaning of money?

11

When Obstinates Attract

Step 10: Form a financial partnership with your spouse.

A good marriage is a lifetime calling to ministry.
—James Walker

Submit to one another out of reverence for Christ
(Ephesians 5:21, NIV).

There is an old bit of folk wisdom to the effect that opposites attract. Like most generalities, it is only partly true. Differences that are attractive during courtship may quickly become fuel for ugly disputes after marriage. Before long, the "attractive opposite" becomes the "detracting obstinate."

In our materialistic society, money is a metaphor. We all know the force that money has, both for good or evil. That potency is obvious, even in marriage relationships. The renowned psychologist H. Norman Wright describes it this way:

> In some marriages allowing a spouse free rein with the finances is extremely threatening. Why? Because to many people, money is an expression of their own independence and power. If someone else has access to their money and a different style of handling finances, there is a definite threat![1]

What can you do if you find yourself in a marriage where money, or the lack of it, is a constant source of friction? What about the spouse who seems unable to control the urge to overspend? The one who is financially irresponsible or can't hold a job? What about the spouse who is stingy? And what about the former spouse who uses money issues to wield power?

Step 10 provides a stepping-stone to marital peace and economic prosperity:

Step 10:
Form a financial partnership with your spouse.

You can begin the process, even if it is one-sided in the beginning. Couples who have applied the principles outlined in these pages have found that their marriages were improved in the areas of

- Restored friendship with each other,
- Improved love life,
- Restored respect for one another.

I had one client tell me, "A good budget can do more for a marriage relationship than a black lace nightgown!"

Bring the Love Back Into Your Budget

Remember the way you used money during your courtship? Regardless of how much there was, you spent the available finances in ways that enhanced romance, created joy and made both you and your loved one feel better about yourselves.

Do you remember how you scrimped, saved and planned in order to buy that special gift? You were budgeting, weren't you? Any type of financial planning that involves action is budgeting. Sometimes budgeting is effective, sometimes not. During the first days of your relationship, you took pains to use your money so love would grow. It can be that way again.

In the following pages we will explore some of the common types of financial communication barriers that plague marriages, and ways to break down those walls to build financial partnership.

The Spouse Who Controls Through Spiritual Blackmail

Healthy mutual submission is a vital component in a workable relationship. We know it is God-ordained because it is a pattern lived out and exemplified for us by our Savior. Jesus demonstrated the correct pattern of leadership by washing the feet of the disciples. He defined His relationship to His followers by stating that the Son of Man came not to be served, but to serve. (See Mark 10:45.)

The woman who wishes to be loved and cherished must be willing to set aside selfish interests and think first of the needs of her husband and children. The husband who wishes to be a leader in his home must also be willing, in a figurative sense, to wash the feet of his spouse and his children. When both parties in a marriage are aligned in this posture, there is no problem too great for them to solve together.

Chuck and Barb Snyder are a many-talented husband-and-wife team who own a successful advertising agency. Their ministry includes their work as chaplains to the University of Washington Huskies football team as well as popular seminars for young couples, where they teach the principle of partnership marriage. They have applied it in their own lives and found it is the secret to long-term marital happiness. Chuck writes:

> I'm not sure just where I got the idea that if a couple cannot agree on something, the man is to make the final decision. I think it came from something I

> learned at church actually. It's so common to equate headship and leadership with decision making. And besides, it's hard taking our wives' counsel. What does she know about advertising, banking, finances, construction, mechanics or whatever the husband does for a living? It is very easy for the husband to get the mistaken idea that he should make all the final decisions around the house if the two partners can't agree. After all, the Bible says the man is supposed to be the leader, right? And that means he should make all the final decisions, right? If it comes to an impasse between the partners, then he casts the tie-breaking vote, right?
>
> Nothing could be further from biblical truth in our opinion. The tragedy is, many evangelical churches are teaching this type of thing. How arrogant to have one of the partners on a fifty-fifty team making independent decisions. No one would stand for that in the business world.
>
> Jesus Christ is our example of leadership. The Bible makes it clear that Christ's headship and leadership in the Church meant He *served*—just as a husband is to serve his wife instead of ruling with an iron fist. If one of the partners doesn't feel good about a decision, or even if one is just neutral, I would not go ahead and do it. It's simple, yet hundreds of thousands of homes are being torn apart by an indifferent, insensitive man who thinks leadership is ruling rather than serving... Both husband and wife gave up the liberty to make independent decisions when they got married.[2]

When a partner makes unilateral decisions the message is, "I don't care about your wishes and needs. You are a non-person in this relationship."

If such messages are given continually over a period of years, deep unhappiness will result, even though the offended party may remain silent. Eventually a divorce takes place. There are millions of these divorces every year—ones we don't hear about. They don't involve lawyers or courts. They are not public. No one packs a bag and moves out. If we could take a survey, my belief is we would find that 90 percent of all marriages end up in this kind of "divorce." These are the separations which are invisible, in which one spouse simply "leaves" by moving to the other side of an invisible, but nonetheless real, island of unfeeling.

A domineering spouse can be wooed to an attitude of servanthood that extends to money matters, but it will take patience. Pastoral counseling should be considered. If your spouse refuses to help, get counseling for yourself. If you are unable to find counseling, there are many fine books on the subject of mutual submission in marriage, several of which are mentioned in this chapter.

In addition, there are helpful books on loving confrontation which will help you communicate more effectively. As Dr. Marjorie Laird says, "Assertiveness is effective communication!" While lovingly claiming your right to be treated as an intelligent adult, pay close attention to the steps given at the end of this chapter. If there are things you would like to improve in your marriage, don't start on your spouse. Start with yourself.

The Spouse Who Controls by Overspending

Susan and Barry were complete opposites. Susan was talkative, outgoing and impulsive. Barry was thoughtful, deliberate and quiet-spoken.

Susan did not seem to have an unusual problem with spending before their marriage. Two years into the marriage, however, she began to exhibit an alarming tendency to make impulsive purchases, particularly for personal items such as clothing.

These shopping forays resulted in bitter disputes. Barry thought Susan was being selfish and irresponsible.

Susan thought Barry was unreasonable and stingy. They were ready for a divorce when they came to me for financial advice.

It was clear to me that their problems would not be solved by my telling them what percentage of their income they should spend on food, rent and luxuries. Their fights over money were really struggles to find out how much (and if) they were loved. A budget would not heal the rift that was forming between them. They agreed to work on the budget I gave them, but at the same time I suggested they seek counseling to find ways to solve their communication problems.

With the help of counseling, they discovered that money could be a symbol of love or lack of it.

Barry learned during counseling sessions that Susan felt abandoned. After a glorious courtship, he now spent all his time working. It was as though, having taken care of the "business" of getting a wife, Barry now wanted to focus all his energy on the next "business"—getting ahead in his career.

In truth, that is the way Barry viewed life—as a series of problems to be solved. He tended to have energy for only one problem at a time. Without admitting it to himself or Susan, he felt Susan should also now set aside the frivolity of dating and romance and get on with the no-nonsense business of life: earning a living, paying bills, cooking and picking up his suits at the cleaners.

When Sanguine Susan tried to view their life together through Barry's duty-sensitive, Melancholy eyes, she became depressed and resentful. He didn't want a wife; he wanted a housekeeper, she reasoned. Why else was he so grim and serious all of a sudden? Where were all the sweet little gifts that had sparked their love in the first place? The flowers?

Susan decided Barry's love for her was superficial.

Without gifts and flowers, she felt like an old, scuffed shoe. Unattractive and unwanted. Taken for granted. In a wash of loneliness and disillusionment, she concluded that if Barry didn't care for her, she would care for herself. She would make herself feel attractive and wanted. She started buying herself little presents. And more presents.

Barry interpreted this spending as an indication that Susan was not concerned about their future. In fact, it was obvious that she didn't really care for him at all! Couldn't she see how hard he was working to make a good life for her? He worked long hours and weekends, coming home exhausted and too tired, even, to make love. And what appreciation did he get for all his dedication? A spendthrift wife who cared more for silly baubles than for her hard-working husband!

Susan and Barry really did love each other, of course. It's just that they lacked good financial and emotional communication. Through counseling coupled with their own efforts and good sense, they changed their lives. They devised a debt repayment schedule, cut up their credit cards and took other positive steps. Their decisive *actions,* coupled with better *communication* through tenderness, openness and receptivity to each other's emotional needs, brought about the healing that was desperately needed in their relationship.

The Spouse Who Controls by Withdrawing

There are many reasons a spouse may refuse to participate in family financial planning. One of these is hopelessness.

Many men, in particular, reach a point in mid-life where they begin to question their own value. They have not achieved the success they once dreamed of. Younger men are edging up the corporate ladder behind them.

Perhaps they feel trapped by educational limitations, family demands or a boring job. These men are prime candidates for heart attacks or extra-marital affairs.

I have counseled with men who are obviously depressed, and who have been in that emotional state for so many years that their entire family, wives included, believed their silent, morose demeanor is their "real" personality. In fact, these men are suffering from chronic depression resulting from years of staring at a future which seems to be not a ladder but a blank wall.

In November 1987, a woman in our neighborhood was shocked to come home from an evening Bible study to find police cars in front of her house and an ambulance parked in her driveway with its red lights flashing. She rushed through the crowd of neighbors gathered on the lawn to find her husband being lifted onto a gurney by paramedics. He had been stricken suddenly with severe chest pains, accompanied by difficulty in breathing. A heart attack was suspected.

The doctors probed into possible causes. All his life he had been in good health. He was not overweight, he watched his diet and he exercised sensibly. Had there been excessive stress? Depression? Gradually, the answers began to reveal themselves.

For twenty-five years he had dutifully maintained a position which he disliked but which paid well. There were times when he would mention how much he would like to make a career change. His wife had always objected. He would lose his pension, she said. He would lose his job security. And the matter was always dropped.

Now, as she wept and prayed, she realized that for years he had been struggling against depression in a career for which he was utterly unsuited, out of a sense of duty to his family.

Fortunately, our neighbor recovered his health and

his emotional well-being, largely because he had a wife who loved him deeply. Today she has a greater appreciation of how career and financial burdens can destroy a "strong, silent John Wayne type." She has taken steps to ensure that material goals never again take priority over the welfare of her husband.

We can help our mates see over or around walls of non-opportunity if we are sensitive to the pressures of their work. This is true whether the spouse is a husband or wife. But in general, I believe that financial or career reversals affect a man more adversely than they do a woman.

A man who is financially defeated feels he has failed in every respect. His sense of well-being and self-respect are intricately tied up with his finances. Take away his dreams, his hope for the future, and you may literally destroy the man.

In our Western culture it is very difficult for a man to seek or accept comfort from other men when he has failed. He certainly cannot turn to his children for solace. So when such a man gets no comfort from his spouse, he is truly, of all human beings, most desperately alone, lonely and self-despised.

A wise woman will find ways to recharge her husband's self-esteem, help him find new direction and reassure him that there is hope. She will continually let him know how much she appreciates his efforts to provide for the family. She will meet his needs in such a way that he will know he is not just a breadwinner, but the centerpiece of her life, just as she should be the center of his life.

Sometimes a spouse will not participate in financial planning because of a fear of arithmetic, a feeling of being stupid when it comes to numbers. Innumeracy, like illiteracy, is a common problem in our society. A person who feels inadequate with numbers may try to cover up that deficiency by withdrawing and acting disinterested.

Whatever the underlying reasons, create a climate in which your spouse is free to be real. Work on emphasizing everything else that is good with the marriage.

If you detect that your spouse is threatened by money and arithmetic, don't push, degrade or intimidate. Quietly, just pick up the reins and move ahead without a show of disdain or superiority. Take over the tedious chores yourself and give your spouse room to blossom in other ways.

A Dilemma of Trust

David and Melissa had very little disagreement over how to spend or save their money. But they did have one major conflict on the subject of tithing, the giving of 10 percent of one's earnings to one's church or another religious organization.

One sunny morning after worship services, my husband Pat and I were chatting with friends in the vestibule when Melissa drew me aside. She told me she had been struggling with terrible indecision for some months. Melissa wanted very much to tithe. David wanted to give just a few dollars a week. Melissa felt that if she pressured her husband too much, he would resent it and might quit attending church altogether.

For several months she had been taking money out of the grocery allowance and secretly putting it in the church collection plate. Now she was facing a dilemma of conscience. She felt she was faced with the choice of either dishonoring a commitment she had made to God or deceiving her husband.

"Do you think God wants you to do something that would break up the unity of your marriage?" I asked her.

She said she was sure He would not want her to do anything of that kind. Melissa paused thoughtfully. "We're really short on cash. If David finds out I've been giving money behind his back, it will hurt him. It may even drive him away from church."

I asked her if she thought God understood her predicament. She said yes, as a committed Christian she was sure He knew her heart.

"Can you find a way to obey God, and still maintain an open and honest dialogue with your husband?"

She said she didn't know how, but she would pray and think about it during the following week.

The next week she caught up with me in the parking lot and excitedly told me what had happened.

"First, I came to a clear decision that I'm not going to deceive David."

"Did you say anything to David?"

"I sure did. I told him I respected his opinions about not wanting to tithe, but that to meet my own spiritual commitments, I'd like to donate some time to the church—doing typing in the office, for instance—without charge, a few hours a week. Or if they don't have any work for me, perhaps I could get a part-time job and tithe my earnings.

"At first he was surprised. I had never really told him how important it was to me to tithe. But when I explained it to him, he understood. He was totally receptive to the idea."

Another woman in our congregation was married to an unbelieving husband who seemed to resent every dollar she put into the collection plate. She did some figuring and found out that she spent $7 a month on magazines and another $25 at the beauty parlor. She told her husband she would like to give up those luxuries and donate the equivalent amount of money. As he saw her follow through with her commitment in the months that followed, he was impressed by her willingness to sacrifice personal desires for a greater principle. He is now attending services with her on a regular basis.

The Dignity of a Personal Allowance

My husband and I are both Cholerics, so we could easily spend our entire married life arguing about who is in charge. Just after we got married, I experienced the first twinge of pain at the marital harness. After years of being a single mother and head of the family, I did not enjoy joint decision-making in money matters.

Like most Cholerics, I can be fiercely independent in some things. So, rather than go to all the "bother" of working with Pat concerning purchases, I began to buy things without telling him. I felt it would be demeaning to plead, argue or convince my husband regarding ordinary purchases. Once in a while he would ask me about the price of an item, and I would fib. Every time I did so, I felt guilty. I was having a tug of war between my conscience and my stubborn independence. The double yoke of marriage was chafing me in the region of my checkbook.

One day I realized that my actions were dishonest and childish. I had always hated deceitfulness in others, and now I could see that these acts of petty fraud were creating a veil of darkness between my husband and me, and undermining my spiritual life as well.

Have you ever noticed how hard it is to confess? I figured my apology would be easier for him to digest if he did not have to swallow it on an empty stomach. So I waited and approached him midway through dinner, after he had complimented me on my fine lasagne. I looked at him tenderly through the flickering candlelight between us. I told him I had been living a little separate life when it came to some aspects of my spending. I told him I hoped for his forgiveness. To my relief, he responded as lovingly as I could have wished.

How lovely, I thought—and served the dessert.

Then I explained that, while I was not looking for excuses, I felt my past behavior was prompted by my need to have some money which was strictly my own, money I could use in any way I chose. I pointed out that he might also like to have a designated amount carved out of the family finances that was his alone. After all, if the children had allowances, shouldn't the adults? He readily agreed.

Then, over coffee, I found out how much alike we are, we two Cholerics. He admitted that he had also been somewhat sneaky about finances. *He was doing it too!* Even though the amounts of money were not large, the fact that we concealed these purchases from each other made them seem dirty and dishonest.

Since that time we have been giving ourselves personal allowances. What each of us does with the allowance is a private concern. It can be saved, squandered or given away. The personal allowance gives each of us a feeling of healthy autonomy without eroding our commitment to each other.

In talking with other women, I have found that lots of them are also caught up in the habit of financial fibbing. Although I haven't talked to any men yet who will admit they ever engage in this practice, I suspect there are one or two who keep secrets from their wives.

Personal allowances can be as generous or as limited as your income will permit. Try using them in your marriage. It can save your dignity as well as your conscience.

The Ex-Spouse Who Controls by Withholding

Money problems don't end with divorce—they just multiply. Just as we communicate through money within a marriage, we continue to do so in divorce.

Nancy was a divorced mother with two young children. She was a new believer, struggling to maintain a home for her children and eager to grow in her new-found relationship with the Lord. One of the continuing problems she experienced was the failure of her ex-husband to pay child support.

"The child support checks are always late. Once Howard didn't pay anything for four straight months. As a result, I fell behind in my rent and almost got evicted from my apartment," she complained.

Making Nancy wait for her child support payments was one way Howard let her know he was still in control, even though ending the marriage was his idea.

Strange as it seems, a divorce situation can be a good opportunity to test our Christian principles. There is not a more trying period in a person's life. The challenge is, can we live out our beliefs in a practical way? If the answer is yes (and it can be), then we can "speak" with our money in a way that will have an enormous impact on others.

If you are a divorced person, particularly a custodial parent, here are some ways you can make money talk in a way that will bless your hearers and yourself.

1. Include the non-custodial parent in important decisions which affect the child, particularly when those decisions involve money.

2. Make sure that the child support is spent on the child or on expenses related to the child. One woman kept a record book of expenses and then

sent her former husband a copy of the way the money had been used. She felt this was appropriate "accounting," and showed the type of respect, cooperation and openness that she hoped to maintain on a mutual basis. While it was not required by law or by the terms of their settlement agreement, this practice brought about startling results. Within a few months, the support payments were coming on a regular basis, problems with visitation had disappeared, and the children were enjoying a better relationship with both parents.

3. When special needs, especially financial needs, arise, discuss them first with the non-custodial parent, not the child.

4. Do not use the child as a go-between, message courier or referee in money matters. Do not complain to the child about the other parent's failure to pay child support on time, etc.

5. Do not make your ex-spouse "pay" for his/her visitation rights. If the support payments are late, do not withhold visitation rights to "get even." Your child may grow up to equate money with love or the lack of it.

Nancy tried every scheme she could think of to make Howard keep current with his court-ordered child support payments. One day she told me she had had enough. She decided to start living by her principles, no matter what he did.

Howard had left her almost two years before, and moved in with his secretary. For most of that time Nancy had been consumed with hate and bitterness. Now she began to try to put herself in her husband's position, imagining how he felt. She concluded that he must feel guilty, lonely and scared. His mixed feelings were being expressed in the way he handled his money.

Nancy began keeping Howard informed of the way she was using the child support money, even when the checks arrived late. She wrote him letting him know how much she spent on the children's clothing, medical care, books and toys.

"When it was his weekend to pick up the kids, I made sure they were clean and rested, that they had the right clothes packed, and that they were looking forward to having a good time with their dad without any guilt trips from me.

"When I started sending Howard a detailed accounting every month of how I had used the child support payments, he called me up and wanted to know what was going on. I told him I knew it was difficult for him to come up with the child support money every month, and I wanted him to know I was aware of this and was using the money wisely for our children. There was a big long silence. I knew he probably was wondering what kind of a trick I was up to. But when I followed through, as time went on, he changed tremendously toward me. He just couldn't do enough for me and the kids. He was just falling over himself to get those checks to me on time."

Later Howard told me that during their marriage Nancy had seemed extremely selfish in money matters, concerned only about having her own needs met. He had often felt he was nothing more than a meal ticket to her. After a few months of seeing his ex-wife's new-found sensitivity and consistency in money matters, he moved into a studio apartment, alone. A few weeks later he and Nancy were discussing reconciliation. They are now together again, working as a team, financially and otherwise. They conduct weekly Bible studies in their home for young couples. One of their most popular topics is financial partnership in marriage.

This story had a happy ending. But I have heard custodial parents, usually mothers, say that they don't want to "force the issue" on child support. In the meantime, they and their children struggle along on less-than-adequate income while the non-custodial parent avoids his or her legal responsibilities to pay court-ordered child support.

If you find yourself in such a situation, you should reflect upon your duties to your children. When the court orders a spouse to provide child support, this money belongs to the child, not the custodial parent. The child support money is not your money; it is your child's money. As the custodial parent, you are charged with the legal responsibility of seeing that the child has adequate food, housing, medical care and supervision. You do not have the legal right to simply give away your child's money.

If you are a custodial parent, practice the steps outlined above. Show love, fairness and complete honesty in your financial dealings with your former mate. If your spouse does not cooperate, is habitually late or has failed to make several payments, it is appropriate to seek legal advice. If you cannot afford a lawyer, you should contact the local office of the district attorney, whose job it is to help you protect the financial welfare of your children.

Advice for the Non-Custodial Parent

If you are a non-custodial parent, you can use your money in ways that will help to build your child's love and respect for you.

1. If you do not yet have a court order, have a clear, written agreement about how much child sup-

port or alimony you will be responsible to pay, and on what date.

2. Make your payments on time. If you find, due to unavoidable circumstances, that you will be late, write a short note explaining the circumstances and inform the custodial parent when to expect payment. Keep a copy of your letter for your own files in case there is any future misunderstanding.

3. Do not draw children into the child support or alimony conflict, if there is one.

4. Do not use money or material things to bribe, buy love, manipulate or undermine the custodial parent. It is not appropriate to unilaterally buy toys, clothes or other items which will create conflict in the child's other family setting. If in doubt, telephone the custodial parent and discuss a purchase before it is made and presented to the child. One divorced father I know liked to take his son out on weekends and buy the boy stacks of punk rock records, knowing the mother disapproved. In this instance, money was used to create further problems. The result was that the child lost respect for both parents due to their continual bickering.

Divorce is an unpleasant reality of twentieth century life. You have the opportunity to demonstrate love and maturity through the way you handle money issues. Your pattern of behavior will have lasting effects on your child. Isn't it important to use this challenge as a testimony to the fact that you are in the care of a loving God?

Marriage Is a Ministry

Marriage is the most difficult of ministry assignments. It is also the task which offers us the greatest opportunities for spiritual growth and joy. James Walker, a staff member with the Navigators, states: "A good marriage is a lifetime calling to ministry. The goal of that personal ministry is to make a significant difference in the life of one other person."[3]

We can help our spouses overcome financial disabilities by the visible demonstration of our faith in the context of our commitment to the marriage relationship. We start the process of change by first working on ourselves.

> What are my husband's greatest needs and how can God use me to supply them? . . . Many women start their ministry with their husbands by hammering away at the needs that the husband would prefer to ignore. As in any other ministry, we should start by first meeting felt needs in a way that will be appreciated. . . . In what ways do I need to grow and develop in order to minister more effectively? People who minister to others should apply the standards they are setting for themselves first. As God supplies our shortcomings our confidence grows that He can use us to meet our mate's needs.[4]

Many women tell me that their husbands are unwilling to discuss money matters. These wives are apprehensive and unsure about how to confront their husbands lovingly on these issues. Usually such husbands are resistant to family or financial counseling as well.

How to make a point to such men? One way to reach an unreachable spouse is through the emotionally neutral process of reading. A particularly helpful book, written by a former certified financial planner, might help your husband get a new slant on the family budget. Dan Benson writes in a down-to-earth style in his book *Man Talk* (Tyndale House Publishers, 1991). In a man-to-man, conversational tone, he helps men see a woman's point of view on money.

If you decide to buy such a book for your mate, don't destroy your good intentions with a brusque "award ceremony." If you hand the book to him while he's shaving and say, "Here, read this. You need it!" the book probably won't get the attention it deserves. It's better to gift-wrap it and present it along with the other loving tokens at the next birthday or special holiday.

Sometimes we think our mates need a good talking to. That may be true. But as experienced chefs know, artistic presentation whets the appetite.

How to Help Your Spouse Find Healing

1. Continue to love your mate and show it.

2. Make sure you are starting the process of improvement in your marriage by working on yourself first.

3. Do not be a facilitator of failure in your spouse. Don't hide the truth, but share the truth in love.

4. Aim for peace and serenity, but if emotional storms occur, don't despair. In an informal survey, a majority of men reported that they did not embrace change until something tumultuous happened—either an emotional upheaval or some other such triggering event. It is seldom that any of us achieves a major change in our attitudes or behaviors without experiencing strong emotions along the way.

5. Don't nag. When you nag you set up a power struggle. The other person, if he has any ego at

all, will vow to maintain his behavior at all costs, because to capitulate would be a form of surrender to the emotional blackmail of nagging.

6. Be neither victim nor harridan. Many spouses are afraid to confront their mates lovingly because they fear verbal, emotional or physical violence. If there is verbal or psychological abuse in your relationship, seek counseling. If there is physical abuse, get counseling—and protection—immediately.

7. Study the financial principles covered in this book, discuss them together and put them into practice.

8. Praise your spouse. If you pay attention, you'll be able to find something every day that pleases you.

9. Fulfill your spouse's needs. You may have to do some checking to find out what they are. *Ask!* Are you withholding approval, praise, sexual affection? Would your mate be gratified if you went on a diet, maintained better grooming or housekeeping? Expressed an interest in his/her job, hobbies or dreams?

10. Connect yourself to the fellowship of people who love God.

11. Be honest. Do not lie, cheat, deceive or steal within the marriage about money matters or anything else. Your own spending, giving and saving habits should be above reproach.

12. Practice ongoing, continuing forgiveness. Most of us want others to pay for their sins and reap the consequences of their mistakes. Yet we pray to

God not only to forgive us, but to "redeem the years of the locust." Forgiveness is the threshold command of God; without it we can't cross over to a place of healing.

13. Accept. We need to accept our spouses as they are, where they are, even while we are letting them know their *behavior* is unacceptable. The words of the hymn are so apt:

    Teach us, O Lord, Your lessons,
    As in our daily life
    We struggle to be human
    And search for hope and faith.
    Teach us to care for people,
    For all, not just for some;
    To love them as we find them,
    Or as they may become.[5]

14. Recognize that forgiveness is a process. Stephen and Janet Bly suggest that the way to hurdle obstacles of resentment and bitterness is to perform loving acts toward the spouse. "You might not feel very loving at the moment . . . but acts of love can help change and replace unforgiveness with true forgiveness."[6]

We need to learn to be "God's person for our mates in this place and time . . . God's love connection to the person we marry."[7]

We can wait for change in many different ways. Our attitude during this period may determine whether the hoped-for change occurs.

> The absolute worst way to improve our mates is to condemn them. Judgment breeds bondage, which brings restraint, causes confusion, paralysis, and pain, makes division, and locks up potential.[8]

In *Free to Soar,* David and Jan Congo cite ten ways

to deal with conflict in a partnership marriage.

1. Both partners need to agree on an appropriate time to work out this conflict.

2. Pick a neutral place to discuss the issue. (Sometimes the home is an emotionally charged arena.)

3. Identify the real issue that needs to be discussed.

4. Affirm that the two of you are united against the issue or wall that is dividing you. Attack the problem and not each other. The goal is deeper understanding rather than winning or losing a battle.

5. Listen to your partner's words and feedback. Example: "What I hear you saying is . . . "

6. Share your own position honestly and clearly, using "I" statements: "I feel . . . " "I think . . . " "I need . . . " Avoid those attacking "you" statements: "You always . . . " or "You never . . . "

7. Attempt to lower your voice one notch instead of raising it two.

8. Avoid the temptation to be historical and bring up past hurts. When you're wrong, admit it.

9. Resist the temptation to yield or withdraw (either emotionally or physically) before a solution is reached.

10. When you have come to a decision, do not raise it again. You're on the same team and have now made your decision.[9]

Marriage: The Ultimate Financial Partnership

When we embark on marriage, most of us do not think of the relationship as a financial partnership. We tend to think of marriage as a romantic physical union and forget that it is a legal and economic merger as well. Yet finances affect every aspect of our lives and our children's lives.

The Bible says, "Can two walk together, except they be agreed?" (Amos 3:3) This is a good question to ask ourselves concerning our financial arrangements. Can you live out the challenge expressed in Philippians 2:3? When this principle is lived out, a highly-energized, vital working partnership will come into existence.

Opposites do, indeed, attract. After marriage sometimes these Opposites become just plain Obstinates. If you are married to an Obstinate, begin the process of seeking change by developing good financial habits yourself.

The way you deal with money can be a potent language to express your love. Start today to use it as a means to build self-respect and mutual joy.

Form a financial partnership with your spouse. You'll find out what love is all about.

$ $ $

Suggestions for Personal and Group Study

Individuals

1. List ways in which you feel your spouse is using money to enhance your feelings of self-worth.

2. Do you believe your spouse is using money in ways that have a negative impact on your self-worth? Make a list of these behaviors.

3. If your behavior is causing your mate pain, would you be willing to discuss your problems with an unbiased third party in an attempt to seek solutions? If not, why not?

4. List some of the ways you have been using money to exalt your own needs above those of your spouse.

5. What steps can you take, beginning today, to change any of the destructive practices you have listed above?

Groups

After each member of the group completes the individual exercises above, share your list with a partner or spouse. Just read your partner's comments. This is not the time to criticize, complain or defend. With your partner's comments in mind, go back and review the chapter on personality types. In light of your partner's personality, what can you do to be more understanding of the difficulties you are experiencing with him/her concerning money?

12

New Beginnings

Step 11: Give to those in need.

We have grasped the mystery of the atom
and rejected the Sermon on the Mount. . . .
The world has achieved brilliance without conscience.
Ours is a world of nuclear giants and ethical infants.
—Omar Bradley

If you give to the poor, your needs will be supplied!
But a curse upon those who close their eyes to poverty
(Proverbs 28:27, TLB).

Now this was the sin of your sister Sodom: She and her daughters were arrogant, overfed and unconcerned; they did not help the poor and needy (Ezekiel 16:49, NIV).

I hope that in reading about the experiences of others and working through the exercises, you have learned a little about the causes of your problems and that you are beginning to see rewards.

But what can you do to make sure financial difficulties won't creep back into your life? How can you be sure you won't retreat to your old habits?

> One reason why these people reverted back to their old behavior patterns is that they misunderstood the full extent of their problem. True, they wanted victory, but they didn't understand how or why God would bring it about. They, like most of us, wanted to

overcome a specific habit—for their own benefit. They wanted to be free of the symptoms of their problem, but did not want a thorough examination that would reveal deeper problems in their lives which they were unwilling to face. The habits themselves were like the tip of an iceberg.[1]

George Caywood, director of the Union Rescue Mission in Los Angeles' Skid Row, has witnessed the effects of uncontrolled behavior—with drugs, alcohol and finances. He describes the journey out of materialism as a trip that begins with an embrace.

> If we are to journey away from materialism, we must first of all embrace God's mercy until our hearts become quiet and we lose the fear of condemnation. Then, because we are not afraid, we can learn a new way of thinking about the material world. Because we think as God thinks in regard to money, we will be free to live in a non-materialistic way.[2]
>
> I felt enormous relief when I read Luke 5:31,32, where Jesus said: "It is not the healthy who need a doctor, but the sick. I have not come to call the righteous, but sinners to repentance." I am grateful for this fact because I am conscious of a deep materialism in my soul that prevents me from being spiritually healthy. This verse says Jesus came for people exactly like me. If you have felt conviction, a sense of sinfulness, in response to this book, remember that this shows you qualify as one of those for whom Jesus came.[3]

Tim Hansel lives with daily pain, the result of a tragic mountain fall which permanently injured his spine. Through the discipline which his physical limitations have thrust upon him, he has learned to value the wonder of the present moment. As he puts it:

> So many people seem to treat their faith as if it were an artificial limb that they strap on each day.

> Though it helps them stumble along, it never really becomes a part of them. Whatever happened to that holy wonder, that appetite for the sacred? Have we grown blind to the sacredness of everyday things and of everyday people? Where is our appetite for stillness which, as T. S. Eliot says, "the turning point, is where the dance is." What are we waiting for?[4]

We have to find out "where the dance is." Or as Brother Lawrence described it, we have to find the inner garden. We may even "make a chapel of our heart."[5]

When we move from the temporary and tangible to the eternal, we move in the direction of discovering what we really are and what we can be. Gordon MacDonald says: "A person shows significant spiritual growth when he finds it possible to admit that he needs a relationship with God in order to be the human being he was created to be."[6]

We yearn to be all that we can be. When we move beyond surfaces to the eternal, we are open to hear God's agenda for us. This is where our next step comes in:

Step 11:
Give to those in need.

It's hard at first to link giving with receiving. We cannot imagine how performing one activity will bring us an opposite result. We all have heard in Sunday school the admonitions to "Give so that ye may receive." We have heard these words so often that, for some of us, they have lost their meaning.

Is giving optional? It might be helpful to consider the results of *not* giving. I was surprised to discover when I began studying to see what God's Word had to say about finances, that the sin of Sodom was not just sexual sin. Their sin was also related to their use of finances.

> Now this was the sin of your sister Sodom: She and her daughters were arrogant, overfed and unconcerned; they did not help the poor and needy (Ezekiel 16:49, NIV).

It seems that when we are unconcerned about those in need, we are in serious trouble!

The Jews have for many centuries practiced the tradition of *tzedakah,* providing for the poor and needy. By the time of Jesus' ministry, *tzedakah* was deeply ingrained in the culture and consciousness of the Jews—so much so that it was taken for granted. On *shabbat* the family gathered around the table for the weekly observance, with candles and bread and wine to embrace the sacred rituals of prayer and thanksgiving. Each person present—children included—placed coins in a basket or bag for the poor. This is a practice that has continued through the centuries in observant Jewish homes up to this day. It is a custom which vividly impresses upon the young their duty to be givers.

The Messiah emphasized to his followers that caring for the needy was more than an act of brotherly love and regard—it was an act of honor to God, a celebration of worship.

It is interesting to note that Jesus did not tell the wealthy ruler to sell his possessions and give the proceeds to Jesus' work. He did not indicate that God would reward him one hundredfold if he contributed to the apostles' support, their missionary outreach or the building of a place of worship. He told the young man to store up treasures in heaven by *giving to the poor.* First the young man was to put material prosperity in its proper perspective by separating himself from it. Only then would he be truly free, and truly fit, to follow the Master. By loosening the grip which "things" have over our lives, we move into a new area of fellowship with God.

The ancient practice of *tzedakah* prompted Boaz to make special provision for the alien woman, Ruth. This brought him manifold blessings. Not only did he win Ruth as his wife—but he and Ruth had a child. Their names are indelibly written in history as forebears of the Messiah.

The apostles, themselves poor, observed *tzedakah* and even had one of their number who was assigned the task of taking up the collection from among them and distributing it to those in need. Caring for the poor was not just a nice thing to do; it was an article of faith.

> If anyone has material possessions and sees his brother in need but has no pity on him, how can the love of God be in him? (1 John 3:17, NIV)

Examples of People Who Live Tzedakah

How can *tzedakah* be practiced? In ways that are practical and personal to the receiver. Money is the usual gift; but where money is scarce, the true spirit of *tzedakah* can be implemented by the use of whatever one has to share of available resources. It may be time, money, service or hospitality.

Minerva and Charlie are a couple who live in Whittier, California. As the homeless problem in Los Angeles began to spill over into the suburbs, Minerva and Charlie began to find ways to be of help. They did not try to solve "The Homeless Problem" by themselves. They just started with one person, one couple at a time. To Minerva and Charlie, the most needy are those who have mental disabilities, and it is to these people that they feel especially drawn. They help them find apartments, work with them to pay their bills, open checking accounts, find public assistance, transportation, food and jobs.

Creig and Debbie live in a port city in Southern California. When he and Debbie were first married, Creig did not believe there was any way they would ever be able to afford to buy their own home. But a mature man in Creig's church felt a call to put his resources to work. He purchased a large lot. Over a period of two years, six couples joined together and tore down the existing structures. Then they worked together to build their own homes. The couples worked together as teams, building first one home and then the next. As a result, six young families now own homes with affordable mortgages through the creative intervention of a man who found a new way to practice *tzedakah.*

Steve is a mechanic who owns his own garage. He always keeps at least one older car in good running condition to loan to people who are temporarily without an automobile. He has been able to loan cars to missionaries on leave, seminary students and people in financial trouble.

Gail saw the needs of people in her community who needed clothing. She, together with other women in her church, organized a clothing exchange in an unused room of the church. Anyone can contribute clean, pressed, wearable clothes, or take the clothing that they find there.

Gail expressed joy when a man, long out of work, came into the church to find a suit, shirt and shoes to wear to a job interview. "He was so overjoyed when he got the job," she said. "We were glad God put us in the right place at the right time."

I think God is ready to put us in the right place, but some of us are unwilling to budge.

In his book *Good Samaritan Faith,* Bernard Thompson describes the kind of Christian walk that will fill us with energy.

> If you want to care for others Jesus' way, begin by reading Matthew 5–7. Then look for opportunities to

live out His teachings in your home, your neighborhood, and in your local church.... Jesus taught His disciples to live such good lives that others would immediately recognize the extraordinary ways in which His followers demonstrated their faith. Instead of letting worldly standards govern their conduct, His disciples' lives should surpass reasonable, socially acceptable codes of behavior. "Let your light shine before men, that they may see our good deeds and praise your Father in heaven" (Matthew 5:16).[7]

By stepping beyond the limits of the customary, the expected, the socially correct, we begin to embrace Jesus' standard for giving. At that point, we experience freedom from materialism. Such a lifestyle may place us out of step with convictions of members of our own religious group. Bernard Thompson writes:

> Certain religious circles today would have us believe that the ideal spiritual life is one where problems are instantaneously solved and miracles never cease. They insist that to be saved means to be safe and opens one up to a charmed life in which anyone who does not prosper and live affluently is not living fully in the Spirit. Perhaps this has been true for some people. It has not been my experience. And according to my limited observations, it does not seem to be biblical. The Bible, above all else, seems to be a book of reality. And reality has the mark of difficulty.[8]

Our new devotion to a lifestyle of giving may put us out of step with the crowd. But that is just where Jesus wants us, next to Him.

Pay as You Go, Pray as You Go

Will it be easy to achieve the victory you want? Management counselor John M. Montgomery puts it this way:

> Fifteen years ago I would never have considered

> the Bible as a financial guide. During the past decade, however, my attitudes and ideas on management and success have undergone major surgery. Since I met Jesus Christ and accepted Him as my personal Savior, I have come to many new conclusions. One of the most important is that I can do nothing worthwhile without God; but with Him I can accomplish things I never would have attempted years ago.... Even if the going gets tough it does not mean that God is not still at work in our lives. If we read the instructions in the Owner's Manual we will succeed and prosper.[9]

There is no simple way to achieve financial success. It is a trip many embark on but few finish. Why? Because they have their eyes on only one goal—to *Get.* The way to permanent financial freedom—real freedom—is to become a Giver. Give personally. Give practically. Give generously. Your heart will be set free.

When that happens, grab your hat. God has hold of you and He never lets go.

$ $ $

Suggestions for Personal and Group Study

Individuals

1. List below the names of individuals whom you know could benefit by being recipients of your *tzedakah*. You may know them by name or merely by sight. They may be close friends or relative strangers. Next to each name, describe the type of giving that would benefit each individual: money, a loving note, a visit, household help, hospitality, etc.

2. Pick one individual from your list. Go beyond the norm in giving that person what he/she needs today.

3. Reflect: Has God put these concerns upon your heart for the purpose of your fulfilling someone's need? Is this His sovereign way of fulfilling your deeper needs as well?

4. Keep a permanent list of your *tzedakah* concerns. Make it a habit to review it daily or weekly; pray about the ways you can give. Respond by prompt action to the answers that God places on your heart.

Groups

1. What have you learned about the relationship between unforgiveness, greed, hidden rage, loneliness?

2. How do these affect debting?

3. How does unforgiveness (of self, of others) affect our ability to be financially free? Describe from personal experience some situations which have revealed truths regarding the connections.

4. What are some ways that individuals in the group can participate together in setting up flexible *tzedakah* programs to work out the command of Jesus to give to the poor and needy?

13

The Law of Liberty

Step 12: Let go of the past and reach out for the future that is yours.

Aim at heaven and you will get earth thrown in.
Aim at earth and you will get neither.
—C. S. Lewis

But he who looks into the perfect law, the law of liberty, and perseveres, being no hearer that forgets but a doer that acts, he shall be blessed in his doing
(James 1:25, RSV).

What does forgiveness have to do with money management? They are closely related. To chart a new financial course, you must release the past. To move forward you must forgive yourself and everyone else.

Forgiving yourself may be the hardest part of the task.

Forgive Yourself Unconditionally

If you are blaming yourself for your past mistakes, this can prevent you from embracing the new future you want to create. No matter how many books you read, no matter how many resolutions you make, you cannot move on. Why? Because blame paralyzes, keeping us from effective action for change.

Until the emotional debris of the past is swept aside, we cannot grasp the new beginnings we desire. That is why our last step is:

Step 12:
Let go of the past and reach out for the future that is yours.

Most of us know it is wrong to judge others but think it is all right to judge ourselves. We wallow in self-blame, refusing to let go of past mistakes. Release yourself from the past so that you can move toward the future that is yours.

Forgive Others Unconditionally

Chances are there is at least one person in your life whom you feel is partially to blame for the present financial circumstances in your life.

If you are married, you probably place some of the blame for your present difficulties on your spouse. Perhaps you have a business partner who squandered or mismanaged assets. Parents who did not prepare you for the realities of adult life. Children who borrowed money and did not repay. Perhaps the economy has played tricks on you and that "other" political party is to blame.

Forgive everyone in your life who has wronged you financially, whether the wrong was committed deliberately, negligently or unintentionally.

Let go of the past.

How Much Are You Worth?

For many of us, the checkbook is a barometer of self-esteem. I have yet to see a person who is insolvent who is not also suffering from low self-worth. If you are broke, chances are you are also *broken.* Broken in spirit, broken in soul.

Unfortunately, we live in a society which often treats "wealth" and "worth" as though the two were synonymous.

We see Donald Trump naming buildings after himself and the message we get from all of the media attention he receives is, "That is a man of great worth." The syllogism goes like this:

1. The possession of wealth attracts favorable attention.
2. Favorable attention means one is valued (held in high esteem) by others.
3. In order to be a person who is held in high esteem by others, I must possess wealth.

In order to be perceived as worthy, we begin to devote ourselves to the acquisition of wealth. If we can't afford to pay cash to obtain the patina of success, we can always pay for it on time with the help of any number of banks who are willing to extend credit on request.

And so the Debting Game begins.

Ninety-five percent of the people who file bankruptcy accumulated their debts by *choice.* They signed their names to contracts, they agreed to pay and later found out they could not do so. Of the million Americans who go bankrupt every year, 99 percent can read, write, add and subtract. Presumably the creditors who loaned them the money can also read, write and do simple arithmetic.

How can so many people be so wrong? How is it possible to be intelligent and yet make such bad choices? We debt in response to our greed, insecurity, lust, envy and a host of other emotional and spiritual ills. But debting only provides a momentary high. When the bills arrive we don't feel so great. When the angry creditors call we feel worthless once again.

One way to discover your real worth is to find out how God feels about you.

Expand Your Spiritual Growth

During financial crisis we sometimes have a tendency to run around frantically in search of solutions and forget about God. What if you do not have a faith, a religion or a spiritual support system? If you are insolvent, you could not pick a better time to start. What do you have to lose, besides your cynicism and despair?

Buy or borrow a Bible and start reading it. Whether you are new to—or returning to—the Bible, start with 1 and 2 John; the book of James; and the Gospels. Contemplate the words of Jesus in Matthew, Mark, Luke and John.

Continue your reading with writers like C. S. Lewis, St. Augustine, Thomas Aquinas or Billy Graham. There are writers of all four temperaments. Find one who speaks to your "condition."

There is a heavenly design for your life. Reach out to claim that gift that is yours alone. Continue to practice the twelve steps to financial freedom that you have begun.

1. Make a written plan.

2. Make a Budget Box.

3. Take the Money Makeover Inventory.

4. Discover your Money Personality.

5. Network with people of opposite temperament.

6. Keep debt below 20 percent of spendable income.

7. Design a plan consistent with your personality.
8. Plan five years in advance.
9. Consider bankruptcy only as a last resort.
10. Form a financial partnership with your spouse.
11. Give to those in need.
12. Let go of the past and reach out for the future that is yours.

As part of the process of getting real with your finances, get real with God. Your finances will improve. And so will much, much more.

$ $ $

Suggestions for Personal and Group Study

Individuals

1. Make a list of individuals who have contributed to your financial difficulties. Describe the specific ways you feel they have hurt you.

2. Take several moments, revisit the pain and then pray for the grace of forgiveness. Release each person specifically for any act or omission which has harmed you, whether deliberate or without thought. Take each person's name to God and, in prayer, free that individual from the bondage of your judgment.

Groups

1. Discuss the following questions: What does forgiveness have to do with letting go of the past? How does unforgiveness of myself tie me to my past mistakes? How does unforgiveness of others tie me to an unproductive, worry-laden past?

2. Encourage group members to share experiences of forgiveness, both of themselves and others.

3. Suggest ongoing journal work relating to the process of forgiveness, seeking first God's forgiveness, then being certain that we have completed this work by forgiving ourselves and forgiving others. Ask if any would be willing to share their journal entries in ensuing weeks.

Appendix A:

How to Balance Your Checkbook

First, let's not be afraid to ask the unutterable question: "Why, oh why, are we doing this anyway?"

Answers to the Unutterable Question

- In order to know how much money is actually in your checking account.
- So that, in the highly unlikely circumstance you have made some sort of mistake(s), you will catch it (them) before your checks start bouncing.
- So you will be sure that the bank has not made any mistakes.
- (less important, but nonetheless valid) So you will feel good about yourself.
- (if you are a Melancholy) So you can sleep at night.

Now that you've sorted through some good reasons for balancing your checkbook and found one or more that will motivate you to the task at hand, let's get on with the dirty details.

Start With a Clean Slate

The process of balancing your bank statement with your checkbook involves comparing transactions over a particular time-span. In order to be accurate, you must begin with a correct balance in your checkbook. You can't let your checkbook go unbalanced for months and then decide one day to balance it by going through one month's checks.

Be sure that your beginning balance in your checkbook (check register) is correct. If you are not sure your beginning balance is correct, wait a week or so until every check you have written has cleared the bank. Then call the bank and get your present balance. That will give you a starting point.

It's helpful to separate the process into two distinct functions.

1. Adjusting the bank statement.

2. Adjusting the checkbook.

After these two tasks are completed, the balance in your checkbook should be the same as the balance on your adjusted bank statement.

The first part of the process is to make sure that the bank has correctly listed all checks submitted to it as well as all deposits you have made. Second, you will want to be sure your checkbook balance is correct—that you have not made errors in subtraction and that you have entered all checks, service charges, transfers to savings and ATM withdrawals.

Look over your statement and make a mental note of the date the bank prepared the statement. Now take out the checks that came with the statement and put them in order by check number. Open up your checkbook so that the check stubs or check register are visible. You will go through your check register two or three times, each time looking for different information.

First, Check Your Bank Balance

On a sheet of paper (or on the back of your statement), write down the "ending" or "present" bank balance as shown on your bank statement. That is the amount the bank says you had in your account as of the date the statement was prepared. We'll call this your "Statement Balance."

Second, Check Your Deposits

Go through the check register to check your deposits. When you come to a deposit that is on your bank statement, write the word *OK* or put a check mark in the check register AND on the bank statement. Check each deposit, continuing through your check register to the present.

If your records show you made a deposit before the bank prepared the statement and it is not listed on the statement, call the bank right away. If your deposit was made *after* the closing date of the statement, write the amount on a list titled, "Deposits After Statement." Total up all "Deposits After Statement" and add this figure to your Statement Balance.

Third, Compare Your Withdrawals

Compare each check stub (or entry in the check register) with the checks the bank has mailed you. Are the amounts written on the check, the amount entered on the check stub (or check register), and the amount deducted by the bank all correct? If so, write *Paid* on the check stub or make a check mark or some other symbol to indicate that the check has cleared the bank. Go through each check in this way. If the bank has made a mistake in reading the amount of any of the checks, call the customer service representative at the bank right away.

You will probably find that you have written some checks which have not yet cleared the bank. Make a written list of these checks, the check number, the payee (person to whom the check was written), and the amount on a list titled, "Outstanding Checks." Add up the total of all the checks you've written which have not yet cleared the bank. Subtract this amount from your Statement Balance. The final figure you arrive at is your "Adjusted Bank Balance." Your bank statement is now balanced.

Fourth, Adjust Your Checkbook

Go to your check register or check stubs and subtract any service charges, transfers to savings account, ATM withdrawals, etc., which you have not previously deducted. If the bank statement shows you made a deposit which you forgot to enter, add that amount. Make any corrections that are necessary.

Now your checkbook is balanced. Your checkbook balance and your "Adjusted Bank Balance" should be the same. If they are not, check your math and watch for any numbers you may have transposed. If there is still a problem, you can go to the customer service representative at your bank for assistance. Don't be ashamed to ask for help. It's not a reflection on your abilities or intelligence. If your bank is not willing to provide you with courteous assistance, get another bank.

Summary

1. Write down your ending bank balance as shown on the statement. You can use the form on the reverse side of your bank statement. This is your Statement Balance.

2. Compare your check register with the deposits shown on your bank statement. Make a list of deposits the bank has not yet entered. Add the total of these deposits to your Statement Balance.

3. Sort your checks by number and compare them with your bank statement and your check stubs

or check register. Make a list of all the checks you've written that have not yet cleared the bank. Subtract this total from the Statement Balance. This is the amount you now have in the bank. This amount is your "Adjusted Bank Balance."

4. Go through your check register and make any necessary corrections. Subtract any bank service charges, ATM withdrawals, etc., that you have not previously entered. Your checkbook balance should now be the same as your adjusted bank balance.

Congratulations! *You've done it!*

Notes

Chapter 1

1. Margaret Truman, *Harry S. Truman* (New York: William Morrow & Company, Inc., 1973).

2. "Whatever You Do, Don't Lose Control," San Bernardino *Sun* (March 5, 1990).

Chapter 2

1. "How to Be a Winner," *This Week* (August 14, 1960).

2. Helen Thurber and Edward Weeks, eds., *Selected Letters of James Thurber* (Boston: Little, Brown & Co., 1981).

Chapter 5

1. *The Oprah Winfrey Show,* January 4, 1990.

2. Florence Littauer, *Personality Plus* (Old Tappan, NJ: Fleming H. Revell Company, 1983); Florence Littauer, *Your Personality Tree* (Waco, TX: Word Books, 1986).

3. David Keirsey and Marilyn Bates, *Please Understand Me: Character and Temperament Types* (Del Mar, CA: Prometheus Nemesis Book Company, 1978).

Chapter 8

1. J. Andre Weisbrod, *Becoming One Financially* (Elgin, IL: David C. Cook Publishing Co., 1989).

2. Chuck Snyder, *I Prayed for Patience and Other Horror Stories* (Sisters, OR: Questar Publishers, Inc., 1989).

Chapter 11

1. H. Norman Wright, *Making Peace With Your Partner* (Waco, TX: Word Publishing, 1988).

2. Chuck and Barb Snyder, *Incompatibility: Grounds for a Great Marriage* (Sisters, OR: Questar Publishers, Inc., 1988).

3. James Walker, *Husbands Who Won't Lead and Wives Who Won't Follow* (Mineapolis, MN: Bethany House, 1989).

4. Walker.

5. *Help Us Accept Each Other,* words by Fred Kaan. © 1975 by Hope Publishing Company, Carol Stream, IL 60188. All rights reserved. Used by permission.

6. Stephen and Janet Bly, *Be Your Mate's Best Friend* (Chicago, IL: Moody Press, 1989).

7. Dr. David Congo and Jan Congo, *Free to Soar* (Old Tappan, NJ: Fleming H. Revell, 1987).

8. Congo and Congo.

9. Congo and Congo.

Chapter 12

1. Erwin W. Lutzer, *How to Say No to a Stubborn Habit* (Wheaton, IL: Victor Books, 1979).

2. George Caywood, *Escaping Materialism: Living a Life That's Rich Toward God* (Sisters, OR: Questar Publishers, Inc., 1989).

3. Caywood.

4. Tim Hansel, *You Gotta Keep Dancin'* (Elgin, IL: David C. Cook Publishing Co., 1985).

5. Brother Lawrence, *The Practice of the Presence of God,*

trans. E. M. Blaiklock (Nashville, TN: Thomas Nelson, 1982).

6. Gordon MacDonald, *Ordering Your Private World* (Nashville, TN: Thomas Nelson, 1984).

7. Bernard Thompson, *Good Samaritan Faith* (Ventura, CA: Regal Books, 1984).

8. Thompson.

9. John M. Montgomery, *Money, Power, Greed: Has the Church Been Sold Out?* (Ventura, CA: Regal Books, 1987).

Index

D

E

F

G

H

I

J

L

M